WOODTURNING
SPINDLE **PROJECTS**

WOODTURNING
SPINDLE **PROJECTS**

ALAN HOLTHAM

GUILD OF MASTER CRAFTSMAN
PUBLICATIONS

First published 2009 by
Guild of Master Craftsman Publications Ltd
Castle Place, 166 High Street, Lewes
East Sussex BN7 1XU

Associate Publisher: **Jonathan Bailey**
Production Manager: **Jim Bulley**
Managing Editor: **Gerrie Purcell**
Project Editor: **Gill Parris**
Managing Art Editor: **Gilda Pacitti**
Designer: **Terry Jeavons**
Photographer: **Alan Holtham**
Illustrator: **John Woodcock**

Set in Adobe Gill Sans
Colour origination by GMC Reprographics
Printed and bound in China by Hung Hing Co. Ltd

Contents

The Turning Workshop

Projects

Introduction

Woodturning has become an extremely popular pastime in recent years and is now a well-established branch of mainstream woodworking. Everybody loves wood and a nicely shaped piece just demands to be touched. It is all part of the psychological property of timber, a back-to-basics instinct that links the world's most natural material to sensual properties that are hard to define.

The real plus for woodturning is that, unlike many other forms of woodworking, it produces a very quick result and shapes can be created for minimal capital outlay on equipment, tools and materials. You don't have to be highly artistic or dextrous either, so it really is a craft that anyone can attempt. If you do get a liking for it, then yes, you probably will end up spending some serious cash, but that can be of your choice, you don't have to.

It is not mastery of technique that hampers the progress of the beginner, but more the lack of inspiration for things to make. For others, although the initial idea is clear it is the various stages of the workflow that are hard to grasp. All this comes with experience and confidence and I hope the projects in this book will show you how to think through the processes and apply them to some ideas of your own. There is a huge range of both functional and ornamental projects you can make. In fact woodturning is now straying down the pathway of art, with many wonderfully decorative pieces that are not obviously turnings but actually have their origins on a lathe.

This book is not intended to be a detailed woodturning instruction manual, although the initial chapters do give some basic guidance on tools and equipment. My aim is to introduce a range of simple spindle turning projects with detailed step-by-step pictures showing the complete procedure needed to make them. The projects are not difficult and should be relatively quick to make, even for a beginner. Woodturning is very easy, providing you grip the work properly and use sharp tools correctly – these two factors constitute 80% of the battle. The remaining 20% is the skill component, it is that easy.

I hope that having followed my methods the first time, you will have gained some confidence and be inspired to try your own. As with many skills there is more than one way to complete the job and you may find a different or easier way that suits you better. Half the fun of woodturning is figuring out the sequence of operations and building confidence.

I have assumed some basic knowledge of tool techniques and finishing, but have covered anything I think to be particularly relevant on each project. As they are all spindle projects there is inevitably some repetition, particularly in the initial stages, but I have deliberately left it this way so that each project is completely stand alone. You can dip in and out at any particular project without having to read the others before it.

At all stages I stress the need for keeping the techniques simple and use the minimum of equipment. The influx of cheap Far Eastern machinery has brought the beginner's woodturning budget well within the reach of most people. You do not need the most expensive lathe, hundreds of tools and a shed full of timber! All the projects in this book were turned with a total of about ten tools and 90% of my day-to-day turning is carried out with just six. In my opinion, manufacturers tempt us to buy more and more expensive tools to try and overcome a particular problem, when in fact the problem isn't there, we just haven't properly mastered the basic techniques with basic tools.

For me, wood is what woodturning is about. It can be very frustrating, cracking and warping when we least expect it, but the thrill of finally mastering it and producing something both functional and beautiful from a gnarled old lump is hard to express, particularly when it invokes a positive reaction from other people as well. Using the lathe to peel back the waste to reveal what lies within is an almost mystical experience to someone like me, who loves wood. Every piece is unique, so treat wood with respect for its amazing heritage and you will be similarly rewarded.

Don't be disheartened by a few failures along the way – we all have them. I have probably made all the mistakes you will make, and often still do, but remember, every day is a learning day.

Enjoy yourselves and keep the world turning!

Alan Holtham

The
Turning
Workshop

Setting up a Turning Workshop

If you are just starting woodturning it is important to make the process as easy as possible and a good start is to set yourself up with a decent workshop of some sort, **❶**. If it is set out properly with all your tools and accessories to hand, there is far more incentive to go out and have a quick turning session, rather than wasting valuable time organizing everything, then putting it away again after use. Apart from the safety aspects, you just cannot be creative trying to work in a disorganized mess. The work area doesn't have to be grand; in fact it is rare that you are able to set up a dedicated turning workshop and the lathe usually comes along as an addition to your existing workshop facilities. Often the lathe is squeezed into a corner, with little regard for its comfortable or efficient use.

This is a shame, because it is the one machine that you will spend more time standing at than any other, **❷**. Working with a bandsaw or planer usually involves just minutes of use, yet you can be stood at the lathe for hours on end. Hence the need to spend some time thinking about the likely work pattern when you are turning, bearing in mind both your personal abilities and what you will be making. In a turning workshop, the work triangle involves lathe, grinder and workbench, all of which should be within easy reach of each other (as shown in **❶** below left), otherwise you will end up walking miles in a normal working day.

If you embrace these general principles, you should end up with a safe and pleasant working environment. My woodturning haven is a little shed at the bottom of the garden **❸**.

GOLDEN RULES

Having set up several turning workshops over the past few years, I have formulated the following golden rules. They are in no particular order, and the list is not exhaustive, it is just based on personal experience.

1 Big is not always beautiful, particularly for woodturning. A small workshop is much easier to control, will save a lot of walking about, and is cheaper to heat.

2 A long, thin workshop is generally more efficient than a square one, especially with regard to the work triangle.

3 Plenty of natural light is essential. It should be supplemented with artificial light, ideally daylight-balanced, with dedicated spotlights on machines such as the lathe.

4 Turning is very messy, so make provision for easy cleaning up. Think about safety, particularly with regard to dust and its extraction.

5 Have plenty of electrical sockets on a properly wired and protected circuit. This will save the time and frustration caused by constantly plugging and unplugging everything.

6 Turning can generate antisocial noise, so consider installing some form of insulation which will also help with heat retention.

7 Think long and hard about your likely work pattern before you start installing machines. Be flexible with the eventual layout and try machines temporarily in place for several weeks before you finalize their position.

8 Think ahead and try to allow for future acquisitions at this stage. Also try and minimize any unnecessary upgrades by buying the right machine – the cheapest is rarely the best, so buy good quality in the first place.

9 Allow for plenty of storage. You will soon accumulate lots of small tools, accessories and gadgets which are easily lost in the piles of shavings. Simple, efficient and visible storage is the only answer.

10 Make sure your workshop is secure against theft. Machinery and power tools are in great demand secondhand, so make sure you keep yours.

The shed is very compact and neatly embodies a lot of the above guidelines. The structure itself is brick, with an inner lining of thermal blocks that have excellent insulation properties. The walls are painted a light colour to keep it brighter, which makes a huge difference with a dark wooden shed. The lathe is sited under a window to give plenty of natural light, ❹, but this is supplemented by four double striplights and an adjustable work light on the lathe. Fluorescent lights are often not recommended for use where there is rotating machinery, as they can apparently have a stroboscopic effect, which makes the spinning wood or cutter appear stationary. Personally, I have never experienced it in 35 years of workshop use and will continue to fit striplights until I find them dangerous, but I do fit daylight-balanced tubes.

Although a swinging-head lathe means that there is no major space requirement at the left-hand end of the machine, if you are going to do any long-hole boring there must be enough room on the right to use the long auger, ❺. Also, remember that the swinging head needs quite a lot of room behind it if you want to swing to the 90° position. This is a situation where using the lathe temporarily in place for a few days will show up any siting problems that are not immediately obvious, ❻.

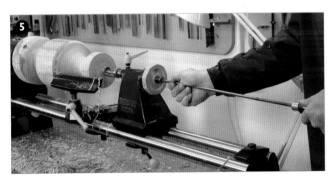

Electrics

To a large extent the siting of the machines will determine where you need to install plug sockets, though if you put in plenty, as I recommend, you should end up near one. If there aren't enough you will find yourself using trailing extension cables that become a real trip hazard. For workshop use I prefer metal-clad sockets, which are much more robust than plastic ones, which are easily broken by stray bits of wood or tools falling about. Being surface-mounted you can put them anywhere. Use plastic conduit to link them together making it is easy for additions or alterations to the system later, ❼.

If you are in an external workshop bring the electrical supply into a small consumer unit with suitable shock protection, ❽. This separates you off from the house and minimizes any interference with each other; putting the lights onto a different circuit from the sockets is also a wise safety precaution. Divide the supply up into several rings if you are going to use a lot of machinery. It is surprising how the power demand builds up as you start plugging in more and more tools, and then add heaters and a kettle!

Storage

Storage is the next consideration, and particularly for turning tools, which take up a lot of space but need to be easily accessible. Mounting them on wallboards keeps them within easy reach, and you can soon see if one goes missing, ❾.

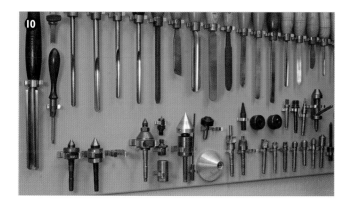

You will accumulate lots of small but expensive accessories and tools, so get these all fixed onto a handy board as well. Mine are within reach of the lathe, so they go straight back onto the board after use, rather than getting lost in the shavings. Once again, any gaps are immediately obvious and you can search for anything missing before it is too late, **10**. Reserve this arrangement for the most commonly used accessories, keeping the rest in the cleaner environment of cupboards or drawers. Chucks in particular need to be kept as clean as possible, or the operating threads soon start to get stiff, **11**.

If you don't fancy making large numbers of drawers yourself, try visiting your local secondhand office furniture shop. They often have banks of small filing drawers on sale for a very modest cost. These are strong metal, but very light and neat, and are ideal for the workshop.

Timber is the other major storage headache and you need to build suitable racking. I have some shelves made from white contiplas for dry blanks **12**, but I use a rack with wooden slats to help with the necessary air circulation for blanks I am still trying to dry. However, provide plenty of support, as timber is very heavy and the weight soon builds up. You cannot have too much timber storage, and it will spread outside the workshop as you get more involved, **13**!

Remember the work triangle, keeping as much as possible within arm's length to save your legs. Sealers and polishes kept on shelving near the lathe may get a bit dusty, but they will then be readily accessible when working.

Heating

Heating the workshop is the one issue on which everyone seems to have his or her own opinion. The romantic notion of using a cast iron pot-bellied stove stuffed full of shavings may seem like a good idea, but it has serious drawbacks. Any form of open flame, from solid fuel or gas stoves, is a real danger, particularly if you use a lot of finishes with flammable solvents such as cellulose. They are also very hard to control and have to be lit each time you need to use the workshop. If you are working in a garage, the ideal solution is running a radiator off the central heating system. Install it with thermostatic valves and you can then leave it on very low to keep the workshop frost-free when you are not using it. Remember that many of the finishes are susceptible to frost.

For other locations I find electric heaters are a safer bet. Fan heaters tend to blow too much dust about, but an oil-filled radiator with built-in timer and thermostat is ideal, ⑭. You can set them to heat the workshop just how you want it even when you are not there, and they are not that expensive to buy or run.

Workbench

Although you won't need a workbench on the scale of a cabinetmaker, you do need to have a clean, flat area to work on. With all the other storage systems in place, it should remain relatively clutter-free at all times and doesn't have to be huge. I keep a small piece of carpet to put on the top, to prevent finished work becoming scratched or damaged, ⑮.

A true workshop evolves gradually over time. In fact it never reaches a finished state but keeps altering as your own demands and working patterns change. However, with a sound framework in place, your workshop should absorb these changes and continue to work efficiently.

Security

Workshops are often sited away from the house, maybe down the garden like mine, so think hard about security. Woodworking machinery and tools are a prime target for thieves. Windows will need locks, ⑯ and maybe even bars or grilles, if you are in a high-risk area. The door needs to be securely lockable either using a mortice deadlock or a heavy-duty hasp and staple with a good-quality padlock, ⑰. Think about fitting a dedicated shed alarm, as well.

Lathes and Bandsaws

Lathes

As a general rule, the heavier and more substantial your lathe is, the better. Vibration is the woodturner's worst enemy, particularly if the workpiece is long or out of balance, and there is nothing to beat sheer weight to minimize this vibration. For this reason, it is better to buy a lathe that is cast rather than fabricated, as it needs to be as smooth and quiet as possible.

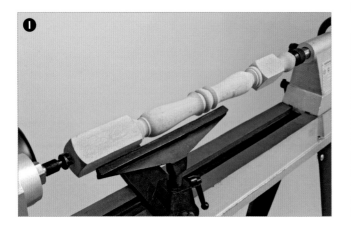

LATHE SIZE

Lathe size is usually measured by the distance between centres. For general work you will need at least 30in (762mm), preferably 36in (914mm), ❶, but whilst a very long bed may appear attractive, it may add to any vibration problems unless it is properly braced. Another useful measurement of size is the 'swing' of the lathe, which denotes the maximum size of work that can be turned over the lathe bed. For serious work, you need a swing of at least 8in (203mm), ❷.

A professional turner will probably need a heavy-duty floor-standing lathe, but for the home woodturning enthusiast a bench-mounted lathe will probably be quite sufficient, ❸. The advantage of mounting it on your own bench means that you can get the centre height just right for you.

Conventional legstands stands vary from a rather crude folded-steel arrangement, ❹, to a more rigid affair with provision for a tool shelf. Bear in mind that the whole performance of your lathe depends on how well it is mounted, so only buy a legstand if it looks man enough for the job. A homemade wooden bench is often better at absorbing vibration than a crude metal stand, and it can change the whole operation of the lathe. If you are short of space in the workshop you can build in a lot of storage under the lathe, which also helps to give the whole structure a bit more mass, ❺.

LATHE BED

For ease of production, the bed is often made from either heavy metal bars or tubes, ❻, but some machines still feature a flat metal bed, ❼. It must be strong enough to support both the tailstock and the toolrest without any flexing, and to allow free and easy movement of the toolrest and tailstock. It must also enable shavings to fall through and sit well clear of the bench, so you can slide the tools underneath it without banging the sharpened edges.

HEADSTOCK

This must be equally solid, ❽. Fabricated headstocks are rarely heavy enough for turning large or out of balance work. Check that the spindle has adequate support in the headstock; some imported models have what looks like a huge headstock, but when you remove the belt cover the two support bearings are actually very close together, ❾. A small bearing spread like this will cause problems with rigidity. Some machines have a taper bearing running in a bronze sleeve, which gives much greater support, but does require occasional adjustment, ❿. The headstock spindle is threaded to take a range of accessories, so choose a standard thread, or you will be limited in the range of extras you can buy. $^{3}/4$in x 16 tpi is becoming the industry standard for smaller machines, with 33in x 3.5 tpi for bigger ones, ⓫. 1in x 8 tpi is more common on a lot of the imported machines, particularly those destined for America.

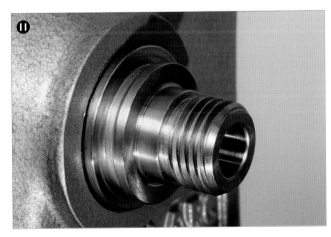

The spindle should also be bored out to take Morse taper fittings. There is a huge range of fittings with this taper and, as it is completely universal, you are not limited to one manufacturer's range. Morse tapers are commonly Number 1 or Number 2 on the smaller lathes, the bigger the number the thicker the taper, **12**. The tapers just push into the headstock and are then knocked out with a bar that runs through the main spindle, **13**. If the spindle is solid, there needs to be a centre ejector which screws onto the spindle nose before you insert the taper, **14**. Take care with these tapers and keep them clean and undamaged, or they will start spinning inside each other, which will lead to inaccuracies when you are using fittings such as drill chucks.

To turn bowls bigger than the swing over the bed there are two options. First, the spindle can be extended through to the left-hand end of the headstock and you turn on this end clear of the bed, called 'outboard' turning. This has disadvantages, one of which is that the spindle thread has to be left-handed so you need to buy two of each chuck. The preferable option is a machine with a swinging head, where the whole headstock turns relative to the bed. You can lock this angled just a few degrees off the centre line and then work off the bed, **15**, or swing it right round 90° to the bed and use the proper bowl rest extension, **16**. Thus, you use the same spindle, but don't have to work left-handed. Even quite large, heavy-duty lathes incorporate this swinging head feature, which is so much more versatile and requires a lot less space, **17**.

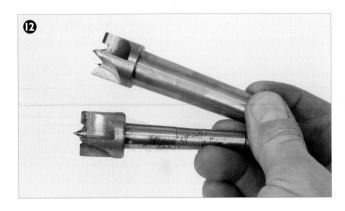

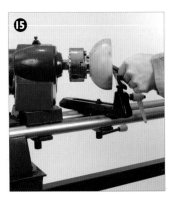

MOTOR AND DRIVE

A small lathe will need a motor of at least ⅓ HP, particularly if you envisage turning large bowls, ⑱, but the bigger the better. In order to give some speed variation, the motor is usually fitted with a three- or four-step pulley, with a matching one on the spindle to give a speed range from about 400 to 2000 rpm. This is achieved with a belt, which is moved around on the pulleys to select the required speed. The traditional Vee belt has now virtually been replaced with the flat poly Vee type, which gives a smoother, vibration-free drive as it has no lumpy joint, ⑲.

Some lathes achieve the speed variation in other ways. This may be mechanically, where a lever operates two cone pulleys, changing their diameter and therefore the speed, ⑳. This system is prone to wear belts very quickly and is quite noisy. Also, you can only change the speed whilst the lathe is running. So, if you finished the last job at top speed and now want bottom, you have to switch the lathe on and reduce speed before you can mount the work.

The ultimate for speed changing is an electrical speed control, which gives you infinite variation of speed at the turn of a knob, ㉑. This does not come cheap though and is usually reserved for the top of the market lathes. It operates by having a three-phase motor fed through an inverter off a single-phase supply.

Whatever your motor type, make sure that the switch gear is easily accessible, and not hidden by large workpieces. I prefer to have the switch, or at least a separate 'off' button at knee height for those emergency situations when you have both hands full. Some machines have a magnetic switchbox, allowing you to move it around at will, depending where you are working, ㉒.

Motors with a reverse facility are a valuable aid for sanding and are quite safe to use on between-centres work. However, if you engage reverse with a piece of faceplate work, there is always the possibility that it will unscrew itself, so lathes with reverse should feature a faceplate locking system, ㉓.

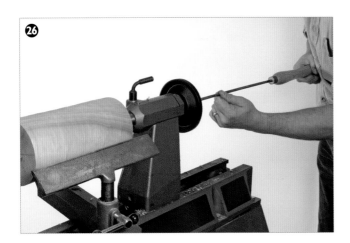

TAILSTOCK

This needs to be as substantial as the rest of the lathe, as it has to provide firm support for between-centres work, **24**. Make sure that it slides freely and locks firmly onto the bed. The tailstock barrel moves backwards and forwards with the handwheel, **25**, and needs plenty of travel for drilling work. The tailstock should be bored with a Morse taper to match the headstock, and also be drilled right through to allow easy removal of the tailstock centres. A hollow tailstock also makes long-hole boring for lamps so much easier, **26**.

TOOLREST AND SLIDE

The toolrest assembly must be quickly and easily adjustable, although the actual locking mechanism varies from machine to machine. Some use a simple clamp and lever under the bed, **27**. As this is operated from underneath, plenty of space is needed under the lathe for hand-free access. Others use a cam type of lock – better as it is accessed from the front, **28**.

The toolrest itself locks into the holder and it is vital that this works effectively. For general use the rest should be about 10in (255mm) long and of heavy-cast construction, so that there is no movement when you are working at the end of it, **29**. Alternative rests should be available with different lengths, and you will probably need a shorter one at some stage.

Bandsaws

The bandsaw is undoubtedly the most useful machine in any woodworking shop, particularly when dealing with large-section material. Even a modestly priced machine will happily cut through 6in (150mm) material. For serious cutting, a two-wheeled machine is essential, as its much larger-diameter wheels can accommodate thicker-gauge blades, which will cut true against the fence and will last without breaking, **30**.

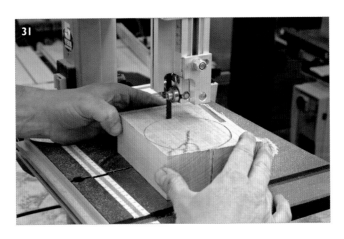

One of the best features of a bandsaw is its relative safety. It is so much safer than a circular or radial arm saw, mainly because all the reaction forces generated by the blade are pushing downwards onto the table, and there is little chance of the dangerous kickbacks associated with other sawing machinery.

If buying a bandsaw, try and decide on the maximum depth of cut you are likely to need, then add a bit on to give you some spare capacity. As the distance under the guides is only the theoretical depth of cut – and may not actually be attainable in some timbers – a bit of spare is needed.

Bandsaws are normally classified by the wheel diameter rather than depth of cut and the smallest machine that will give a creditable performance is a 10in (255mm), **31**. This will take thicker blades and rip true to a cutting depth of about 4in (102mm). If you want to rough out turning blanks this capacity isn't really enough and the next stage up is a 12in (305mm) machine that will reliably cut 5in (125mm) material and up to 7in (178mm) at a pinch, **32**. If you anticipate doing a lot of re-sawing, or perhaps small scale-conversion of logs, then the next stage up is a 14in (355mm) machine which will give you an 8in (203mm) cut for very little more money.

If you are a serious woodturner continually handling big, heavy chunks of timber, then the ultimate is a heavy, cast-iron machine with something like 18in (460mm) wheels and a 12in (305mm) depth of cut, **33**. Everything on a machine like this is bigger and stronger and built to withstand some punishment, but trade the cost of all this off against the amount of use when you are working out your budget.

Chucks and Accessories

Faceplates and screwchucks

There are of course many situations where you cannot hold work between centres, as you need free access to one end of the workpiece.

The conventional holding device in this case is a faceplate and in fact a lot of flat work is still called faceplate turning, even if it is actually held by some other means, ❶.

Faceplates come in a variety of sizes but for general use a 4in (100mm) version is most useful, though think about adding a 6in (150mm) if you do a lot of big bowl work. Although a faceplate is very simple, it is important that you buy a good-quality one. I prefer a machined-steel one with a short boss, as this should run true and is less likely to distort than an aluminium one, ❷.

An even more useful device for holding workpieces is the screwchuck, and I would rate this as the number-one lathe accessory. Again available in various sizes, this is essentially just a small faceplate with a fixed central screw, the common sizes being 1^1/2in (38mm) and 2^1/2in (63mm) diameter, ❸.

A standard screwchuck should take normal woodscrews, so you can replace them as they wear and, for maximum versatility, you need to be able to vary the amount of protrusion of the screw from the chuck. If you are on a limited budget get a 2^1/2in (63m) screwchuck with additional screw holes, as you can then use this as a small faceplate as well, ❹.

The one disadvantage of both screwchucks and faceplates is that they are both 'invasive', in that you are left with screw holes as a permanent reminder of the holding method.

In the case of the screwchuck you have to part off clear of the screw, which can be quite wasteful as well, ❺. Nevertheless, both faceplates and screwchucks are essential lathe accessories and you will need to use both at some stage, no matter what type of woodturning you are into.

Scroll Chucks

A more expensive long-term answer is to buy some form of woodturning chuck, and the scroll chuck has become the most popular type, mainly because it is so simple to operate, ❻.

This style of chuck has revolutionized the work-holding process and has simplified most woodturning operations. There are many different models available from a range of manufacturers, so if you are bewildered by the choice, stick with one of the well-known makes and you won't go far wrong, ❼. They are all basically the same as regards function, the main differences being in the range of additional jaws that are available.

Scroll chucks work on a similar principle to the engineer's self-centring chuck, where an internal threaded scroll draws all the jaws together simultaneously. The scroll is operated with either a hexagon wrench or a more conventional chuck key, ❽. The main advantage of this is that you can open and close the jaws one-handed, so the chuck can be left on the lathe as you hold the work with one hand and tighten the chuck with the other, ❾.

Lathes all seem to have different threads on the spindle nose and the various manufacturers obviously have to accommodate this if they are to make their chucks universally acceptable. Some actually offer the chuck with the back bored to a specific thread, whilst other manufacturers overcome the problem by boring the chuck body with a single large thread and then supplying a range of inserts to suit the various lathes, ❿.

❼

❽

❾

❻

❿

The big advantage of the threaded-insert arrangement is that you can update to a different lathe without having to reinvest in a new chuck – you simply have to change the insert, which will cost just a few pounds rather than the hundreds necessary for a new chuck, **⓫**.

The lever-operated versions are a halfway house in the world of scroll chucks. Instead of the single chuck key providing the jaw movement, this type uses two levers, **⓬**. This is cheaper to produce and also results in a beautiful slimline chuck with very little overhang. The big disadvantage is that it requires two hands to operate, so the work therefore has to be mounted horizontally whilst it is off the lathe, **⓭**.

The one thing all of these chucks have in common is that they form the basis for a huge range of different jaws, **⓮**. The jaws are normally fixed to the chuck with a couple of small machine screws and each jaw and carrier on the chuck is numbered, so it is good practice to fit the right jaw to the right carrier, **⓯**.

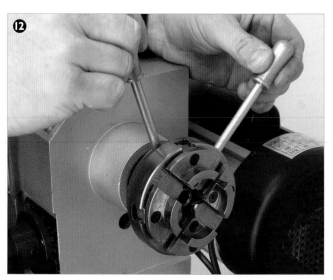

The range of different jaws available is often very extensive, but do not be tempted into buying too many at the start. Some of them have distinctly specialized applications that you will probably rarely use, and you are far better waiting until you find a definite need for a particular jaw type. Unfortunately there is no standardization here and all the manufacturers produce their own jaws; these are not interchangeable and once you have bought into a chucking system you are stuck with it, so choose carefully at the beginning.

Most chucks come with a mid-range set of jaws, usually in the region of 2in (50mm) in diameter. This is actually the most useful size and will cover a vast range of work. Remember that with a scroll chuck the same jaws are used for expansion and contraction, so if you're making a bowl you have the choice of turning a dovetail recess in the base or forming a spigot and the same jaws are used for both, ⓰. This is a significant advantage over most of the other chuck types that require separate jaws for expansion and compression modes.

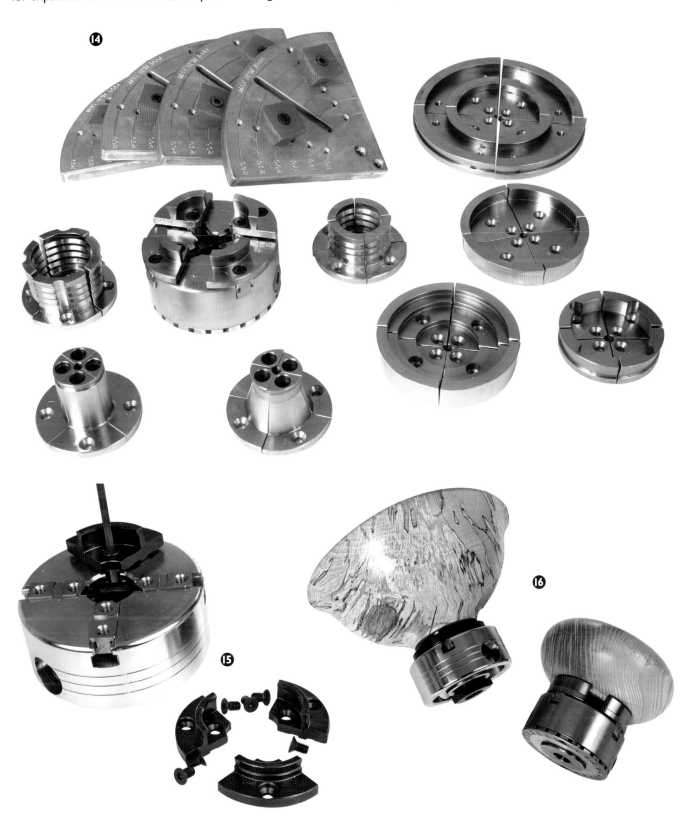

These chucks are not restricted to faceplate work either. You can use them to grip round stock, so you can either hold a complete cylinder, or turn a gripping spigot on the end of a bigger-diameter piece, **17**. I regularly use my scroll chuck for holding square work as well, **18**, which is particularly useful if you're gripping something like a table leg or stair spindle that incorporates both round and square sections, and where the centring is obviously critical, **19**. Gripping the square timber in the chuck is guaranteed to give perfect alignment, whereas relying on getting it spot on using a drive centre is less so. However, the jaws may mark the square section slightly which may be a problem.

I particularly like the 'shark' jaws which have a very deep gripping surface. This is ideal when you want better access to the rear of the work but they are particularly good at holding very long workpieces which are unsupported at the tailstock end, **20**. Provided you have made the spigot nice and parallel and the shoulders are slightly undercut the grip is amazingly firm and rigid, but it will highlight any slackness in the lathe bearings!

The standard pin chuck is well known as a means of holding pre-bored work, but it does rely on very accurate drilling for a secure hold. The use of pin jaws on a scroll chuck obviously allows you to vary the diameter of the pin and the drilling becomes far less critical, but the hold is more secure. Like many of the jaws this set is multifunctional, in that there is also a dovetail machined on the end, so they can be used in expansion mode in the bottom of a very tiny bowls, **21**.

If you do a lot of bowl work it is worth investing in a set of the large jaw plates. Used in conjunction with adjustable plastic buffers these are an excellent way of holding finished work without marking it, **22**.

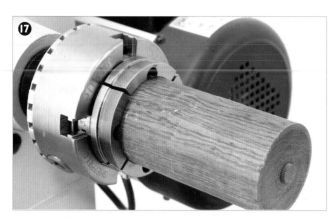

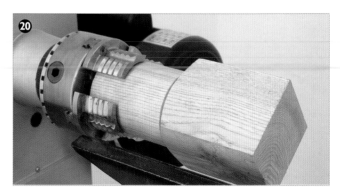

Some chucks incorporate a dividing head in the backplate – one of those features that you use a very rarely, but very handy when you do need it, **23**.

For the initial holding, while you turn some form of chucking recess or spigot, a woodscrew chuck is quicker and easier to use than the conventional faceplate. Even very large, irregular workpieces can be held on a heavy-duty machined screw, and these are usually supplied as standard with a scroll chuck, **24**. Provided you drill an accurately sized pilot hole to accommodate the screw, it has a very powerful hold, but use it in conjunction with some large jaws to maximize the support. With some chucks you can even buy jaw plates that allow you to make and fit your own wooden jaws, if you have a very specialized application.

Other accessories

REVOLVING CENTRE
I would also recommend that you buy a revolving centre if your lathe is not supplied with one, **25**. Standard dead centres have a habit of burning the work, particularly if you are a bit nervous and over tighten them. A revolving centre is relatively inexpensive and you can tighten up the tailstock as hard as you like without having to worry about any danger of overheating.

DRILL CHUCK
A drill chuck on a Morse taper allows you to do a lot of boring work on the lathe. It can be used in either the headstock or tailstock and needs a capacity of at least $^1/_2$in (12.5mm) to take the standard range of sawtooth and auger bits, **26**.

LAMPS
For lamps you will need a long hole-boring kit. This consists of a hollow centre, a counterbore tool and the long auger which is normally $^5/_{16}$in (8mm) in diameter, **27**. If you can find a kit based around a revolving hollow centre, so much the better, but they usually have a fixed centre, so use it with care, or again you will burn the work, **28**.

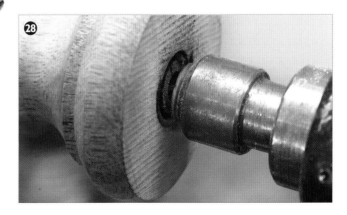

Tools and Grinders

Tools

If you are just starting out in your woodturning career, the huge variety and cost of woodturning tools may all seem a little daunting. However, like a lot of hobbies, woodturning can be as simple or as complicated as you want to make it and you can get started with a really simple kit.

Always remember that turning techniques are highly individual and what suits one person may not suit another. I shall, however, recommend some basic tools that are essential, no matter how you work, ❶. The other tools can come later as you develop your own technique. There is no strictly right and wrong way to turn – as long as you are cutting the wood as cleanly as possible and getting a good finish, it doesn't really matter which tool you're using.

There are several major turning-tool manufacturers, and whilst they all sing the individual praises of their tools, I think there is probably very little to choose between them, provided you stay with well-recognized makes. In fact, because they all produce different profiles suited for particular techniques, you'll probably end up with tools from a variety of sources, ❷.

The main difference is in the handles, which often vary tremendously, ❸. This variation in shape may not appear significant, but as you have to hold the tool for considerable periods of time, it is important to find a design that is comfortable for you. If you want totally unique handles, some manufacturers will supply tools unhandled, allowing you to make and fit your own.

Nowadays there is a vast selection of shapes and sizes of tool, as well as different types of steel. High-speed steel (HSS), with its superior edge-holding qualities, has virtually taken over, mainly because it is very difficult to damage by overheating during sharpening, ❹.

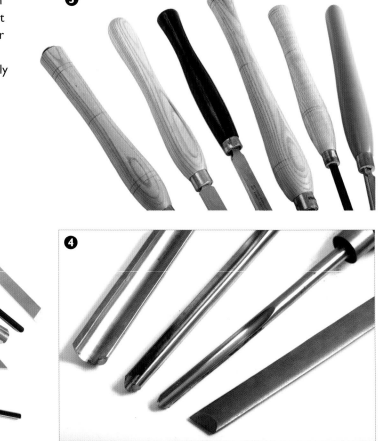

The old carbon-steel tools, while superior in the quality of edge that they will take, are very easily damaged by heavy-handed grinding and their edge will only last a very short time, particularly if you start turning some of the more abrasive exotic hardwoods, **5**.

New materials, like powder technology, cobalt coatings and tungsten carbide, have all found niche markets, but HSS remains the most popular. The dilemma you may face is whether to buy tools individually or in sets assembled by the manufacturer, as many now put together sensible sets containing a range of useful tools, and their attractive price means that this may be a very good way to start your collection, **6**.

When you are looking through the racks of tools at your local dealer don't get sidetracked into buying any of the specialized tools that have been developed for unique applications. These should be bought when you need them or, more importantly, when you know how to use them, but before you get to that stage you have to master the basics, **7**.

You will quickly realize that every woodturner has his or her own ideas about what constitutes a basic kit of tools. There is, however, almost universal acceptance of the six essentials, which are a roughing gouge, a parting tool, $^3/8$in (10mm) and $^1/4$in (6mm) spindle gouge, a skew chisel and a bowl gouge. Some form of scraper, probably a $^3/4$in or 1in (19 or 25mm) round-nosed, will be the next purchase.

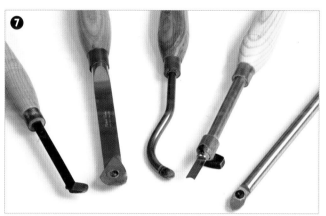

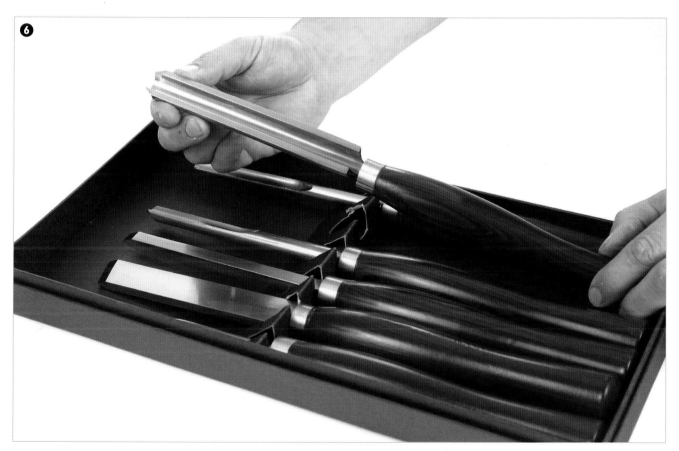

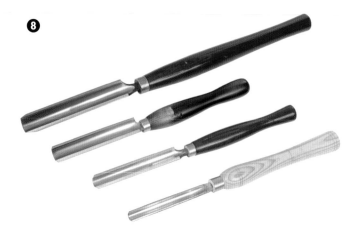

The six essential tools

ROUGHING GOUGES

These come in many sizes from the massive 1½in (38mm) versions for really heavy spindle work, down to a tiny version for miniature turning, **8**. The curvature of the gouge may also vary but it is well recognized that a ¾in (19mm) deep-fluted gouge is the most useful, **9**.

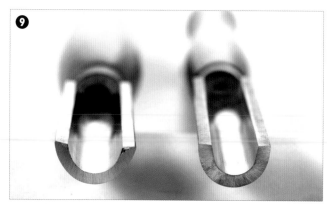

PARTING TOOL

For cutting through or forming shoulders, a parting tool is the next essential; some are much wider than others whilst more expensive versions may have flutes or a diamond section, **10**. For starters, a parallel section ⅛in (3mm) tool will do all your parting work with a minimum of waste, **11**.

SPINDLE GOUGES

Not only do these vary in size, but there are two distinct manufacturing methods used to produce the tools. Until relatively recently, gouges were always forged by hand from a flat bar, to form uniformly thick tools characterized by a tang that fits into the handle. This hand-forging process is obviously a skilful and therefore expensive process. The advent of HSS has meant that a lot of tools are now ground from solid bar, a much quicker and cheaper process, **12**. These round bar tools are quite satisfactory and, in fact, most spindle gouges are now of this section.

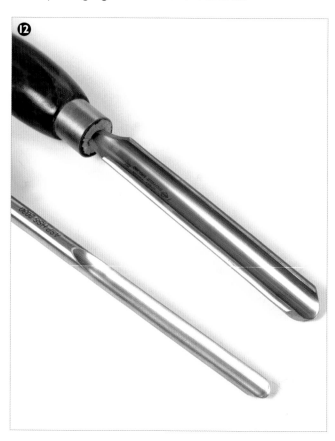

SKEW CHISELS

These have also had something of a modern update. The traditional flat skew chisel, so feared by most beginners because of its undeserved reputation for digging in, now has a more user-friendly brother in the form of the oval skew, which has a curved profile and rounded edges that slide much more easily along the toolrest, **13**.

BOWL GOUGES

These are similar to spindle gouges in that they, too, are ground from round-section bar, but in this case the internal profile is different and is much more U-shaped than that of the spindle gouge, **14**. They are also much longer and stronger to withstand the greater forces generated during bowl turning.

SCRAPERS

These are always looked upon with some contempt by pro woodturners. This is mainly because, although they are very simple to use, they have been mis-used over the years, for performing the wrong function and on unsuitable timbers, the result being torn out or massively bruised fibres that are almost impossible to finish, **15**. However, scrapers do have a real place in your tool kit and provided they are used properly and only at the appropriate time, the results are quite acceptable, **16**.

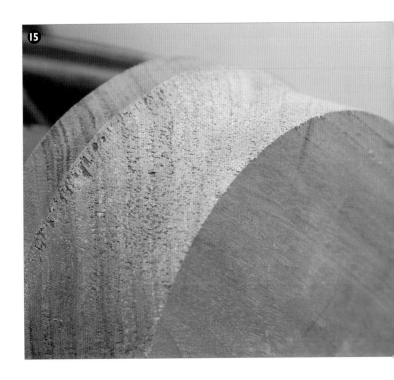

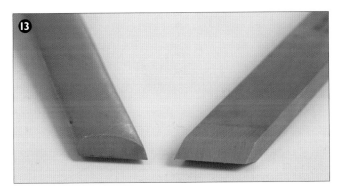

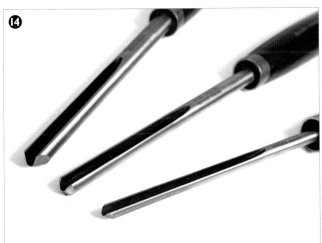

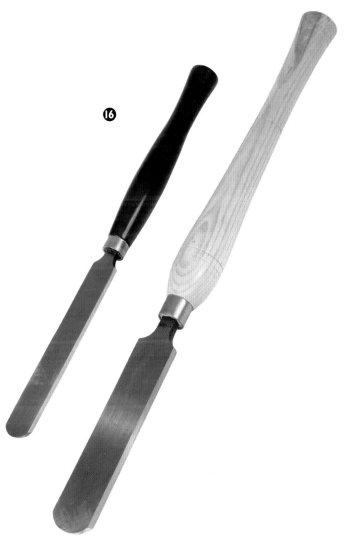

Grinders

Of course, any cutting tool has to be sharp to perform properly and woodturning tools will require more sharpening than any others. Imagine how much wood is passing over the cutting edge when the timber is revolving at 2000 rpm: it has to stand up to miles and miles of continuous use. A grinder of some sort is therefore essential and most woodturners use a standard double-ended version for the majority of sharpening. The good news is that nowadays you don't have to spend a fortune to get a very serviceable machine, but you do need one with wheels of at least 6in (152mm) in diameter and as wide as possible.

This is where the cheapest ones differ from the more expensive ones, as they frequently only have very narrow wheels that make the grinding process a bit trickier to control, **17**. Better-quality grinders will have much wider wheels and the composition of the wheel may also be better. White wheels are renowned as being more suitable for sharpening HSS tools, **18**.

As you will have to use the grinder regularly, it is important that it is located near the lathe, or you will spend a lot of time wandering about the workshop.

However, just having a grinder is not the end of the story and for it to work effectively the wheels must be cleaned regularly by dressing and for this you will need a dressing stick, sometimes called a devil stone. Holding this against the revolving wheel cleans off all the impregnated metal and exposes a fresh surface that will grind more quickly and without overheating, **19**. You cannot use a grindstone without a dressing tool, so make sure you buy one with the grinder.

Unlike most other woodcutting tools, it is unnecessary to hone woodturning tools. The wire edge formed by a fine grinder is sharp enough for most purposes and, in fact, you often do more damage to the edge trying to sharpen it further with an oilstone. However, certain tools like the skew chisel may benefit from a little light honing with a fine slip stone, **20**, but don't overdo this, and be prepared to regrind them regularly.

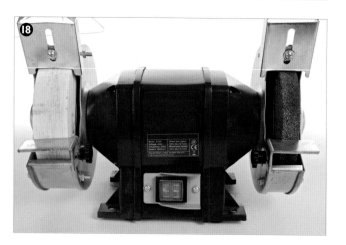

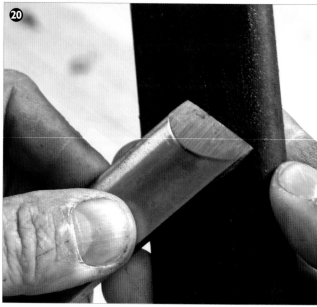

Because it is so easy to overheat the tools using a fast-running dry grinder, the wetstone type may seem like a better alternative. Whilst these are superb for sharpening, producing a really keen edge with minimal loss of steel, they tend to be slower to set up and it is relatively expensive to buy the full system, **21**.

Many professional turners will sharpen the tools freehand on the grinder and, whilst this may look simple, it has often taken many years to perfect the technique, **22**. For the speed and convenience that professionals need, it is worth them developing the necessary freehand grinding skills.

However, like many things, it is actually quite simple once you get the hang of it but, if you are still struggling with sharpening, there are now all sorts of jigs available to help you get a professional-looking grind, **23**. Some of these are easier to operate than others, so try and arrange for a demonstration of a particular jig before you buy it.

There are, however, some jigs that are so simple to operate that even the seasoned professionals are now finding them useful, particularly with the more involved grinding profiles required on some of the latest tools, **24**.

Abrasives

I t is sometimes assumed that the finish will cover up any blemishes left on the surface, but actually it just serves to highlight them. It is therefore essential to spend some serious time and effort with abrasives, methodically working down the grades to produce a perfect surface, otherwise you will never get a good finish. The trick is to try and achieve the best possible surface straight off the tool to start with, always using super-sharp tools and applying them correctly, ❶. Sanding is time-consuming and messy, so do whatever you can to minimize it by turning properly in the first place, and take sensible precautions to protect your health from the dust, ❷ (see pages 46–8).

Abrasives are now available in a huge range of different grades, materials and qualities and like any other cutting tool it is the characteristics of the sharp edges that determine how well and quickly the material cuts.

They all use abrasive particles of some sort which are bonded onto a backing material, usually paper for hand-sanding sheets, or cloth for use on power tools.

The particles sizes are graded into 'grits' and numbered using one of two different classification systems, the lower the number, the coarser the grit size. 'Closed coat' abrasives have closely grouped particles for fast sanding, whereas 'open coat' ones have larger spaces between the individual particles of grit, so that the paper is less likely to clog.

Types of abrasive

All sorts of materials are used to make abrasive paper, though the traditional yellow glass paper has, to a large extent, been superseded by other more modern abrasives, many of them manmade, though they are all still collectively known as 'sandpaper'.

Garnet paper is very hard, with long-lasting, sharp cutting edges, for use specifically on timber. It was widely used before the introduction of the more modern abrasives, the open-coat variety being ideal for sanding turned work.

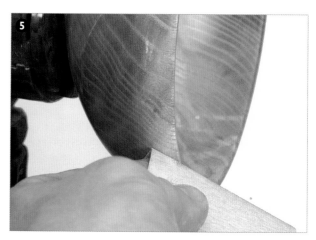

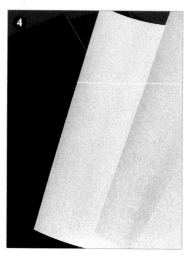

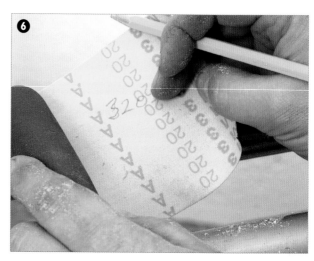

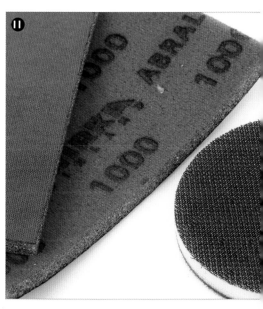

Aluminium-oxide paper is even harder than garnet and is produced in sheets for hand work, but is also widely used as an abrasive for power tools, ❸.

Silicon-carbide paper is another extremely hard abrasive material; available down to very fine grit sizes, it comes in sheets that vary in colour from dark grey to black, ❹. It is a manmade abrasive mainly used for fine finishing on wood or metal, often using water as a lubricant, and is consequently referred to as 'wet and dry' paper. For woodworkers, there is also a pale grey variety, which is treated with a coating to act as a dry lubricant. This makes it ideal for bringing the surface down to a superfine finish, particularly on polished surfaces, ❺.

The back of every piece of abrasive should carry all the necessary information regarding grit type, size and the backing material. However, when you tear up a larger sheet the grit size may be lost, so it is worth marking the back so that you don't pick up the wrong grade, ❻.

Abrasives are available as sheets, rolls, strips and pre-cut discs, ❼. I use a mixture of all of them but you may find it less wasteful to buy abrasives in roll form. More demanding applications, like turning, really require cloth-backed material, which can be folded into a tight crease for detail work, without breaking off the backing, ❽. A new material called Abranet has an open-mesh backing which is extremely flexible but, more importantly, allows the dust to disburse rapidly, which greatly increases the life of the material, ❾. This is fast becoming my abrasive of choice, because you can either use it wet or dry, it is very flexible and it just seems to last forever, ❿.

Velcro-backed and hook-and-loop material is also available in strips and rolls to use for hand sanding, or on small discs for power sanding. This may also be supplied on a sponge backing, to form a comfortable soft pad, ⓫.

The correct procedure for working with abrasive paper is to start with a coarser grit and then work down through the grades until the wood is as smooth as you want and there are no visible scratches. Deciding which grit to start with is something that comes with experience and knowledge of the particular timber you're using, but a common mistake is to start with a grit that is too coarse, thinking it will work faster. In fact this just leaves deep scratches that are almost impossible to remove and you actually end up generating yourself a lot more work, ⓬.

Work progressively down through the grades, rather than leaving a big gap between each successive one. As a general rule, start faceplate work at around 150 grit and spindle work at 240 grit, though there are exceptions to this. At the lower end of the grit scale keep the progression between grades quite close, for example use 100 followed by 150, 240, 320 and finally 400. If you use bigger jumps, it is difficult to remove the fine scratches left by the previous grade, but the effect is far less marked with very fine grades, so it is quite acceptable to move from something like 4000 to 6000 in one jump.

Don't use a worn piece of a coarse grit thinking it will act as a finer grade. Worn abrasive consists of blunt particles, not finer ones, and you then have to press on much longer to have any effect, and also risk causing severe scratching. The burnishing effect of worn abrasive also generates excessive heat and may crack or glaze the surface, making it difficult for subsequent grades to work properly.

Because of the speed of rotation, heat is easily generated, so the first step in the sanding process should be to reduce the speed of rotation, as this will not only reduce the frictional heat, but also allow the abrasive to clear and maximize its cutting efficiency.

Where possible, the abrasive should be held underneath or at the bottom of the revolving work, so that any sudden snatches will not result in painful bent fingers. This is not always possible when you are trying to sand into detail, **❸**, but be aware of the potential dangers and never wrap the abrasive around your fingers – always hold it in such a way that it will be snatched out of your fingers in the event of a catch.

Power sanding is a technique used on larger faceplate items and has several major advantages. For a start the effect is much more aggressive, so the sanding process is quicker and easier, **❹**. Also the spinning abrasive disc doesn't leave the characteristic circular scratches you get by simply holding a pad of abrasive onto the spinning work.

These are available in different sizes and hard or soft configurations. They have a Velcro face which enables you to attach discs and swap them around very quickly, **❺**. My personal preference is for the slightly tapered pads, as these allow much better access and a hexagon shank for a more positive drive in the drill, **❻**. The hexagon shanks can also be easily extended to reach into deep turnings using standard bit extensions, **❼**.

Various self-powered versions are available, which rely on the rotation of the work to turn the disk and so they are not as aggressive as the powered versions, which can be used in a contra-rotating mode for quicker stock removal, **❽**.

Finishing

I t is essential that the surface of your turning is properly prepared before you attempt to apply any type of polish. There is a popular misconception that the finishing stage is the easiest part of the job, and that the polish covers up any faults or blemishes.

In fact nothing could be further from the truth and I often spend as long preparing and finishing a piece of work as I do on the turning stage. Remember it is the quality of the finish that will be the yardstick for the workmanship, not how long it took you to make.

Even a superb piece of turning will be spoiled unless it is finished properly, but the polishing process takes time, so don't spoil it all by rushing. Thorough preparation with abrasives is the key to achieving a truly satisfying finish, ❶.

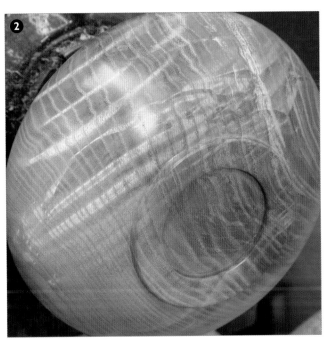

Sealers

The unique feature of a piece of woodturning is the sheer variety of different grain surfaces exposed, all of which have different absorbency rates. If you put polish straight onto this raw wood, it will end up looking patchy, as it soaks in so unevenly. The first stage is to apply some form of sealer to try and even out this differential absorbency. There are two types of sanding sealer, the most popular being cellulose-based.

CELLULOSE

This is very quick drying and provides a durable base, but it is not very pleasant to handle – particularly in a confined space – and it is also highly flammable. Nevertheless, used with care it is an excellent first step in most polishing processes. Cellulose can be applied with a brush or with a cloth. I prefer, to use a cloth, as you can rub it well into the timber surface. To achieve the best result, do this with the lathe stationary, ❷.

CAUTION

When applying finish with a cloth to an item on a spinning lathe, there is a danger that the cloth will become caught up. This risk is minimal provided you are careful, but there are special safety cloths available which tear apart very easily if they do happen to get caught, ❸. A cheaper option is to use kitchen roll, but some of these paper products can be quite abrasive and may mark the surface.

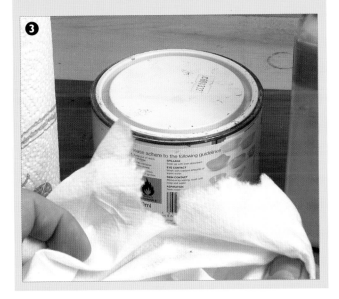

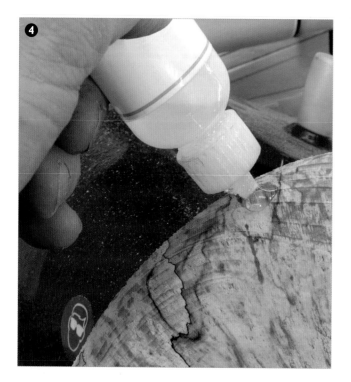

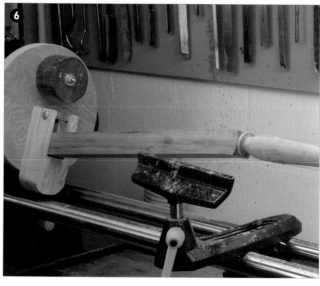

On a very porous piece of timber, such as spalted beech, cellulose sealer on its own may not be enough to stabilize the very soft patches. In this case flood in some very thin superglue to harden it up before you start the sanding process, ❹.

The solvent in cellulose sealer gradually evaporates, so you will need to thin it down on a regular basis using cellulose thinners, ❺. Only thin sealer can properly penetrate the timber – if it is too thick you end up with a surface coating, not a seal.

SHELLAC-BASED SEALER

This does form more of a surface coating and is better suited for furniture work. It takes longer to dry, and subsequent coats can end up dissolving away the first one, unless you apply it very carefully. It is, however, far less toxic and it is a good choice where you want a high-gloss finish on square-section pieces that cannot be finished on the lathe directly, ❻.

There are now numerous water-based acrylic finishes, including a spray-on acrylic sanding sealer, ❼, though personally I still feel that the sealer needs to be worked into the surface by rubbing with a cloth. Spray application inevitably ends up with a surface coating rather than a penetrative one.

Melamine

For a more durable surface, with some nominal water resistance, cellulose combined with melamine makes an excellent finish. This can be applied either with a brush or with a cloth, and again dries very quickly, ❽. It will withstand regular handling and even wiping with a damp cloth, but it is not waterproof.

Lacquers

For a high-gloss finish combined with resistance to handling, some form of lacquer may be more suitable, ❾. Lacquers are available in liquid form for applying with a brush, or aerosol form for quick spraying. The acrylic-based lacquers in an aerosol are easier to use and are less toxic than the conventional solvent-based finishes. The spray also allows you to cover intricate detail more easily.

Friction polish

This is a shellac-based product, normally applied to the work whilst it is spinning on the lathe, to produce a super-high gloss, ❿. These polishes have a high solids content and need to be shaken very thoroughly before use to ensure even mixing.

Friction polish works best over a sealer and I find cellulose sealer makes the perfect base, provided it is flatted down thoroughly. However, it is only really suitable for small items as these can be coated quickly and evenly before the polish has a chance to dry, ⓫. If you try and apply it on large items the polish tends to pull into streaks or rings, because the speed range is so different across the width of the work. Although friction polish can be burnished to a high gloss, the finish is not durable and quickly dulls down if it is handled a lot, so it should be reserved for small ornamental items only.

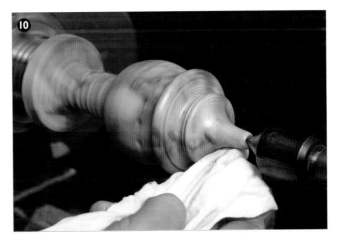

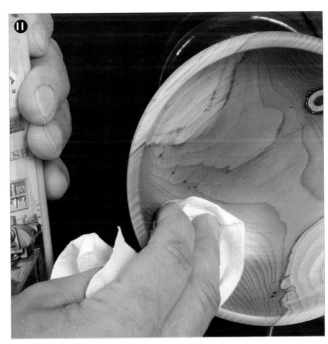

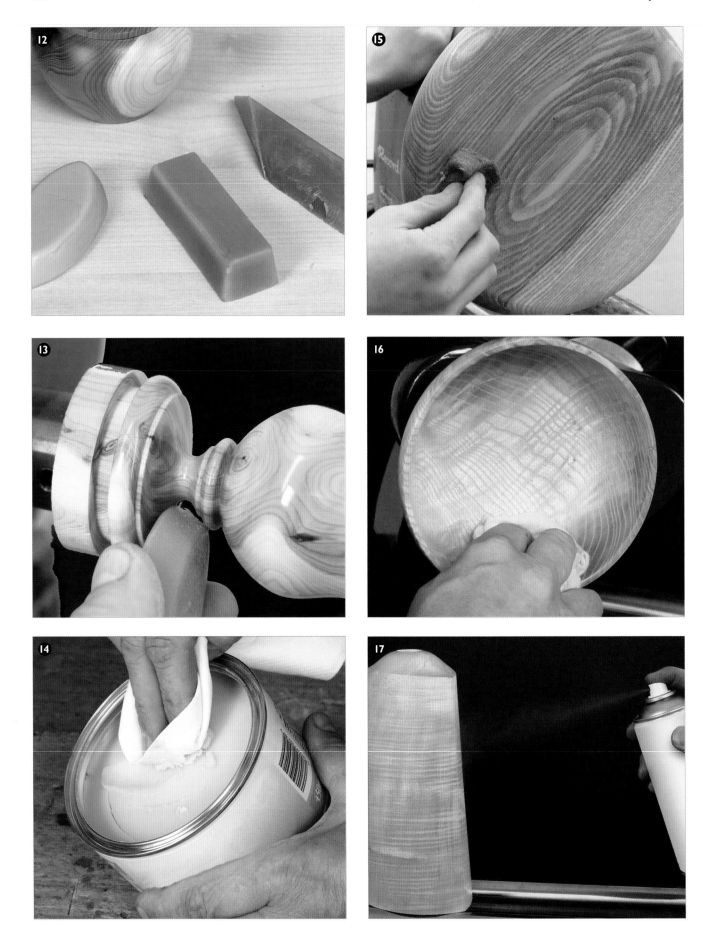

Waxes

These are perhaps the most traditional of finishes and there are all sorts of different blends available. Solid blocks of wax have limited uses for the woodturner. The most traditional form is pure beeswax, but this is really too soft for use on its own and tends to leave a rather sticky, dull finish.

Carnauba wax, on the other hand, is very hard and, although it is capable of producing a really high gloss, it does require careful use to avoid scratching the surface as it is applied to the revolving timber, **⑫**. I often apply pure carnauba wax on top of friction polish to give a richer, more durable shine, **⑬**. You may like to experiment by blending different amounts of beeswax and carnauba wax together to achieve a slightly softer stick that still produces a good shine.

Some waxes have solvents that help them spread and dry quickly and also make them more durable. The soft paste waxes, **⑭**, can be spread easily on the spinning work, ideally using a pad of fine steel wool, **⑮**, and then buffed with a soft cloth to a rich shine, **⑯**. Some of these waxes are now available with natural oils as a solvent; although more pleasant to use, they can be much slower to dry and don't polish up to quite the same degree of shine. Others are available in aerosol form, **⑰**, which makes application very much easier, particularly if there are large, flat areas that cannot be buffed on the lathe. These are perfect for uneven surfaces like burrs, which need some form of shine but are impossible to access with a cloth, **⑱**.

No matter which form of solid wax you use, careful buffing is required to maximize the shine, but they do leave the surface with a wonderful feel.

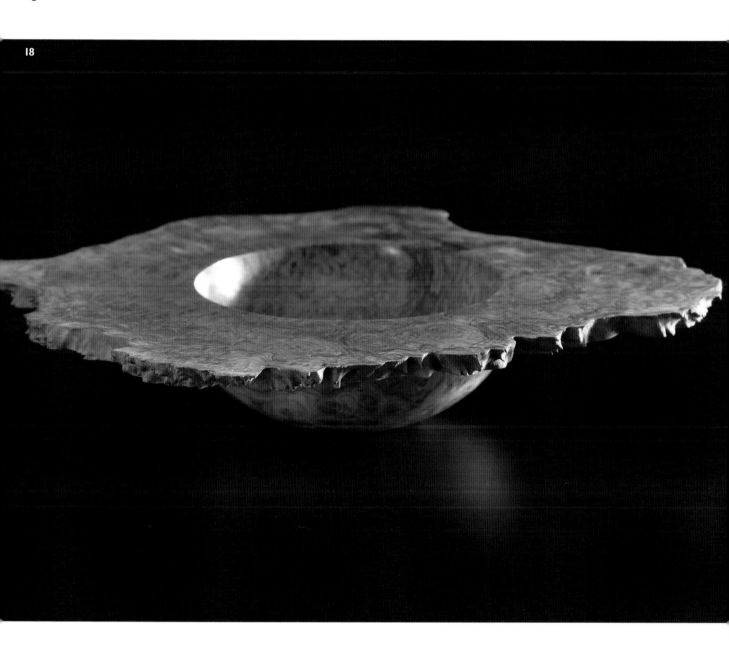

18

Oils

Oils are slightly different, in that they penetrate the surface to a much greater extent, **19**. The various types may have different properties, but all will need several successive coats brushed on to build up the durable finish. If you sand between these coats with very fine abrasive paper and then buff off the final one with a soft cloth, you should achieve a lustre that brings out the very best in the grain without being too overpoweringly glossy.

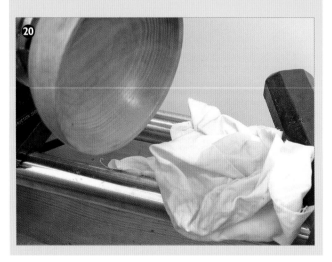

DANISH OIL

This is perhaps the most popular oil finish, containing chemical driers to make sure the surface hardens relatively quickly. Like all oil finishes, it darkens the timber quite considerably. The first coat is often disappointing, as it disappears into the surface leaving a rather patchy appearance, but keep going with several more coats and you will achieve a natural-looking lustre.

MORE NATURAL OIL

There is also a range of more natural oils, such as citrus or eucalyptus but, although these are more pleasant to use, they rarely develop such a high gloss as the manufactured oils. There are other specialized finishes available for use with items that will come in direct contact with food.

COOKING OILS

You can of course use standard cooking oils like sunflower, which is very much cheaper and perfect for items such as salad bowls, **21**. However, these oils will rarely produce any discernable shine and are usually reserved for more utilitarian items. Also, they have no driers or preservatives and have the potential to go rancid if the item is not used and re-oiled on a regular basis.

Specialized finishes

There is also quite a range of more specialized finishes for particular applications, **22**. For instance a black lacquer is available for ebonizing timber – a couple of light coats are all that is necessary to blacken the surface but not totally hide the grain.

For a waterproof seal, suitable for a vase, the best product is plastic coating. This is also proof against alcohol and heat and leaves an incredibly durable surface. It is a catalyzed lacquer, so you have to mix the two components before use and, once mixed, the product has to be used within hours, although you can extend the working life to a few days by keeping the mixture in the refrigerator, **23**. It does, however, leave a rather artificially glossy, almost plastic-like appearance to the timber surface, even if the shine is cut back with fine steel wool, but this is the only product I know that has complete resistance to liquid.

Small items can be polished by buffing on a polishing mop which is charged with either wax or a special polishing compound in block form, **24**. You just hold work against the rotating mop, moving it around to even out the shine. This is a perfect way to get a high-gloss finish without any of the tiny rings or polishing marks associated with conventional polishing on the lathe.

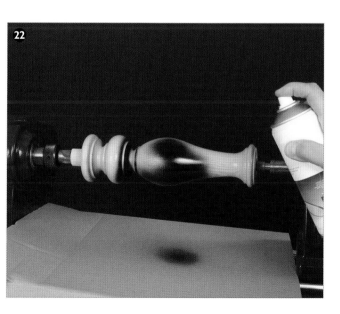

Safety

There are many different aspects to safety in the turning workshop and the potential dangers should not be underestimated. Most are pretty obvious and a healthy dose of common sense coupled to a basic respect for moving machinery will minimize any risk.

No matter what the scale of your workshop, it needs to be neat and well organized, ❶. Apart from avoiding the waste of time involved in searching through piles of shavings for a missing tool, or the risks involved in stumbling round accumulations of timber, you can be much more relaxed and therefore more creative in a tidy environment.

Dust safety and control

Safety in the turning workshop has always centred on the potential dangers of the lathe itself, but now the main emphasis has switched to the less obvious hazard of dust. It is becoming apparent that this can be quite a serious threat to health, mainly because the effects are cumulative and serious symptoms only start to show when it is too late.

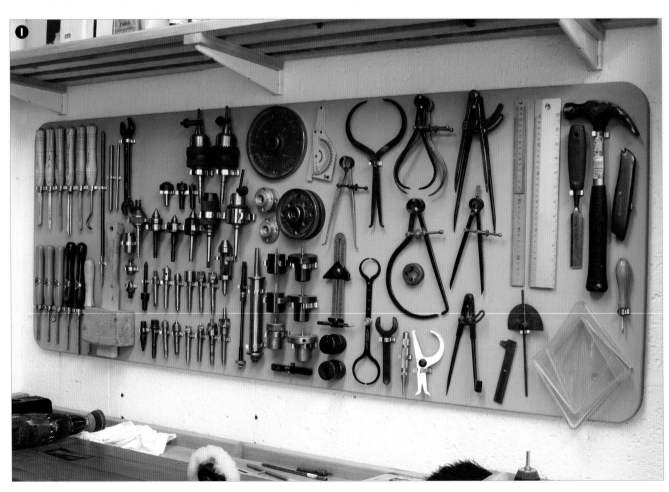

The small amount of dust produced during the actual turning operation is relatively minor, it is only when you start sanding that the levels become hazardous. It is the size of the dust particles that is the key. Very fine dust accumulates in the lungs and is not expelled by the body's normal defence mechanism. Over time this can lead to serious problems and for this reason it is imperative to extract the dust at source as it is produced.

DUST EXTRACTORS

A standard dust extractor with a top filter bag is relatively useless in this situation, ❸. These machines are really chip collectors designed to move the huge volumes of air necessary to extract from a saw or planer. To achieve this high airflow, the top bag has to be porous, so whilst this efficiently retains sawdust or shavings, the really fine dust passes straight through and back into the workshop atmosphere.

If a bag extractor is your only choice, buy a fine filter cartridge to replace the top cloth filter, ❹. This will retain a lot of the finer dust, apparently down to single micron-sized particles. Alternatively, site the actual extractor unit outside the workshop, bringing in the pipe from outside, though this has the effect of extracting your heat as well.

A more efficient solution is to use a vacuum-type extractor, ❺, which incorporates several layers of filtration down to fractions of a micron. These work on high pressure rather than high volume, so you have to get the collection spout really close to the work for effective dust control. I bolt a large crocodile clip onto the end of the pipe and then just clamp it to the lathe bed, ❻.

You can even pipe in a fixed system if you get serious about your turning, ❼. However, no matter how good your extraction system, it is not the complete answer. The movement of the abrasive paper, coupled to the fan effect of the workpiece, means that dust is always diverted away from the extractor nozzle.

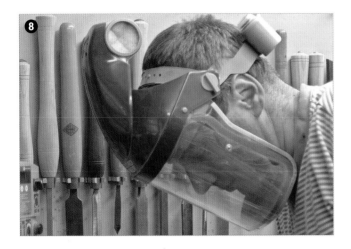

DUST MASKS

For total personal protection, you also need a dust mask. The simple cloth ones that fit over your face are not very efficient and soon become uncomfortable, and the rubber respirators are even worse. You cannot beat an air-fed helmet, which supplies you with a stream of clean filtered air, **8**.

Good though these are, they only protect you personally, they don't have any effect on the general air quality. What is missed by your extractor is left to settle on any horizontal surface within the workshop and shelves soon become covered in a deep layer of fine dust, **9**, which as well as being unhealthy presents a real fire risk. The ultimate protection for this airborne hazard is an air filter which sucks in the ambient air, and cleans it through a filter, **10**. I have one mounted above my lathe and it is amazingly efficient, provided you remember to clean the filters occasionally.

In combination, these strategies ensure that you have as much respiratory protection as possible from dust. Those with skin allergies, however, may still experience dust-related problems, though it is usually only specific timbers that cause these problems.

Fire hazards

The dangers of fire in the workshop are often underestimated; it is not until you see it at first hand that you appreciate how quickly and easily it can occur. My most serious fire encounter involved nothing more dramatic than the grinder and wire wool, **11**. Few people realize that wire wool is extremely combustible. A single spark into a handy bundle soon has it burning fiercely, so keep it well away from the grinder.

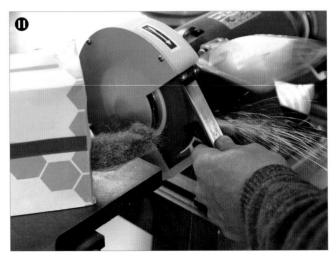

Many polishes, sealers and waxes are extremely flammable, too, and ideally you should keep them in a fireproof store outside the workshop.

This is probably not feasible in a small workshop, particularly as many of them are susceptible to frost as well, so just remember that they are there and take suitable safety precautions.

Accumulations of dust are also a real fire hazard, and relatively small concentrations of very fine material in the air are enough to form an explosive mixture. Fire will also run along dust-covered shelves, so an air filter (see ❿) and good general housekeeping will contribute a lot to fire safety.

If the worst does happen and you do have a fire, an extinguisher may prevent a small incident becoming major. In my own workshop I have a water extinguisher for fires in wood and a large CO_2 one for electrical and solvent fires, ⓬.

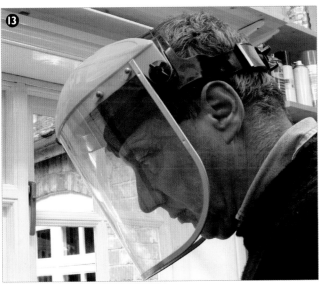

Personal safety

The rest of your personal safety is covered with a good first aid kit, again strategically placed. I also have a handy eyewash bottle filled with clean water for that tiny speck of wood that somehow finds its way round your safety glasses.

EYE PROTECTION
Some form of eye protection should always be worn when turning. This can be safety glasses, goggles or a full-face visor that gives you impact protection as well, if something comes off the lathe at speed, ⓭. Choose what is most comfortable for you, particularly if you are already a spectacle wearer. As I now have to wear glasses for fine work, I had my prescription made up into proper safety glasses by my optician for a very modest cost, but you can also buy off-the-shelf bifocal safety glasses in a range of magnifications, ⓮.

HEAVY-DUTY RUBBER MATS
Fine dust on the floor can make it very slippery, particularly if the surface is painted and, if the floor is concrete, it can also be uncomfortable to stand on for any length of time. Overcome these problems with heavy-duty rubber mats by the lathe, ⓯.

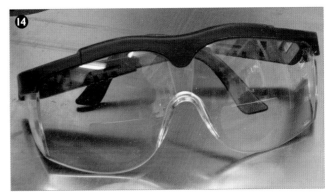

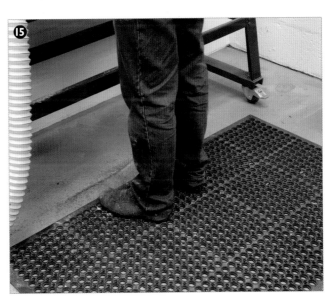

MOBILE PHONES

Woodturning is a rather solitary occupation, so consider having some form of communication with the outside world in case of real emergencies. Mobile phones make this a lot easier, but a simple cordless phone with an intercom to the house is a good idea if you are in an isolated workshop down the garden.

Electrics

Electrical safety is another important issue. It is amazing how many powered pieces of equipment are needed and most workshops have far too few plug sockets. The temptation is to use lots of extension cables trailing all over the floor and, as well as being a real trip hazard, these carry all the dangers of electrical overloading.

TIP

Install plenty of sockets, properly wired in on a ring main, with sufficient capacity for all that you have as well as some spare capacity. In a rugged workshop situation it is best to use the more robust metal-clad sockets, **16**, but fit plenty.

16

Machine safety

The more likely causes of danger involve getting yourself caught up in the revolving workpiece, particularly with sleeves and long hair. If possible wear a proper turning smock with elasticated cuffs which leave nothing trailing even if you get right against the work, **17**. A similar problem also arises with polishing cloths, which can so easily get snatched out of your hand if they wrap around the drive centre. Some people advocate the use of safety cloth or kitchen roll which just tears away in this situation, **18**, but I find this too abrasive for fine polishing and prefer to use proper cloth, with care.

Tool rests are another source of danger, particularly if the work still has corners on it. Right from the beginning, get into the habit of switching off the lathe when you need to move the rest, 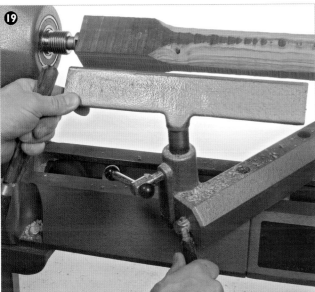, and always make sure that it is tight before switching on the machine. Roughing out a blank is one operation in particular which causes enough vibration to loosen the rest, and the consequences of the rest turning into the spinning workpiece could be dangerous.

In cases of emergency, you need easy access to the off button. This is often located on the motor itself, 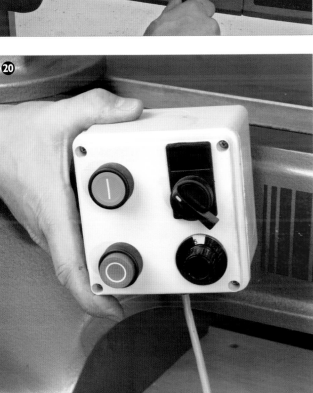, though a more prominent emergency button is preferable,

particularly if you can hit it with your foot. On some machines you can move the switch box to the most convenient place.

Other problems can occur if you start up at the wrong speed, and this is becoming more of a problem with the introduction of the mechanical variable-speed headstocks, which need to be reset whilst running, . You must remember to drop the speed before mounting the next piece of work.

Finally, remember that your finished design may incorporate fine edges which in fact can be razor sharp, and the slightest touch on these revolving knife edges can leave a nasty cut,  – so they are not as innocent as they appear.

Choosing Timber for Turning

Having finally chosen and installed your lathe and its accessories, the time has come to get turning and for this you obviously need some timber. But, all is not as simple as it seems in the world of wood. There are many variables with this most natural material and you can become disappointed and frustrated if all your best efforts are thwarted, not only by your unfamiliar tools or faltering technique, but by the very material you are trying to fashion.

However, if you follow some basic rules, you can minimize the problems and in reality you can make the timber side of woodturning as simple or as complicated as you want. But beware, the whole process of gathering and preparing your own timber can become almost as obsessive as the process of turning it on the lathe!

Buying blanks

The easiest way to acquire wood is to simply go to a specialist retailer and buy ready-prepared blanks off the shelf, **❶**. These are usually perfect as regards quality, and should be dried to a state that allows them to be used immediately. They may appear expensive at first glance, and you might be reluctant to spend a lot of money in the early stages of your turning career. However, bear in mind that you are paying for the waste material that has been cut away to prepare such a perfect piece, as well as the storage and drying time – all very significant factors, as you will find if you start preparing your own.

Beginners are often recommended to start by buying cheap softwood to practise on, **❷**, but this advice must be tempered with a note of caution. Softwood is notoriously difficult to turn well, even with years of experience, and it is easy to become disheartened if this is all you use. Certainly don't spend a fortune on highly exotic blanks until you have become reasonably proficient, but do buy some cheaper prepared blanks of sycamore or beech. Although relatively plain as regards figure, these turn really well and you will soon be experiencing that wonderful 'hiss' as a sharp tool peels away the shape, **❸**. This will inspire you to continue, whereas the torn and dusty grain of softwood will not.

If you are an occasional turner, you can quite happily spend your turning career using ready-prepared blanks. However, once the bug has bitten and your demand for timber becomes more voracious, you will probably want to start sourcing and preparing your own stock. This may not be a much cheaper route, though. If you price in all the time and costs involved in finding the raw material, handling it, cutting it up, drying it and then throwing half of it away, the shop-bought blanks are not that overpriced after all.

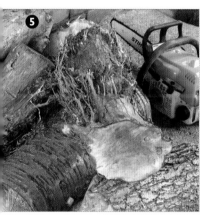

Preparing your own timber gives you much better control, as you can cut the sizes you need in the way you like. But, while it is eventually less expensive in monetary terms, it takes a while to get there and, because converting and drying timber is such an inexact science, the only true guide is experience.

Tree surgeons

Tree surgeons are a good source of timber, as they often deal with more unusual varieties and are glad to get rid of what they regard as waste material. Such small garden trees and prunings are a rich source of decorative material, and thin branches of species such as yew and laburnum, ❹, can be worked in the round, but they have to be dried thoroughly before they can be used.

In order to convert the larger trunks into more manageable pieces you will need to invest in a small chainsaw. I use an electric one around the workshop and a bigger one outside for larger branches, which makes short work of slicing up the wet trunks, ❺. Alternatively, even a small bandsaw will cope with a lot of the conversion work, ❻, just make sure that log sections are securely held on the table and never try to cross cut logs, or they will roll dangerously.

Seasoning

Fresh-cut wood like this contains a huge amount of water and, although very easy to work in this state, it will subsequently crack and warp; the water, therefore, must be removed before the wood is ready for using, which will involve the difficult and lengthy process of seasoning.

You can store small log sections to dry as they are, a process that will take several years to complete. They will crack and split on the end, often to quite a depth, particularly on fine-grained ornamental species like laburnum, ❼. You can minimize this splitting by coating the ends with some sort of sealer to slow down the drying process. Hot paraffin wax is the traditional method, but you can also buy liquid wax to brush on cold and this is much easier to use, ❽.

Another way of seasoning your own timber is to rough-turn it whilst wet. In this process you turn away a lot of the waste timber to the approximate shape of the final item, ❾. This way you minimize the amount left to dry, which significantly speeds up the seasoning process. Even with this method, the ends need to be sealed thoroughly and you will still get failures.

The amount of water contained in even a small piece of wet timber is quite amazing; in reality it is just like a sponge. A moisture meter will give you an immediate reading, **10**, but bear in mind that this is only accurate at the point of penetration of the probe, it may be much wetter further in. A more accurate but less immediate answer is to keep weighing the blanks until their weight remains constant. Although at this point they are not necessarily dry, they are in equilibrium with their surrounding environment.

Remember the sponge analogy: wood will soak up water from the atmosphere if it is wet, as well as releasing it when conditions are dry.

It is very difficult to beat nature by speeding up the drying process too quickly, so you just have to be patient. The ideal drying situation is a cool, shaded area where there are no dramatic or sudden fluctuations of temperature. Somewhere sheltered outside will remove the initial moisture, but then the timber should be brought inside to finally condition it, **11**.

The only possible short-cut for the home seasoner is to try microwaving turned items, **12**. You can do this in a normal kitchen microwave but only use it on the defrost setting. There is no recognized technique for this yet, so you will have to determine your own method, but my limited experience indicates that many short blasts of a minute or so over a period of several hours does the trick. There will be more failures than with other methods of drying, but it is a real short cut if you are prepared to take time to master it.

Avoiding cracks and splits

The process of drying timber often builds up huge stresses within the cell structure and these may show up in a board as major cracks and splits, often severe enough to almost divide it into two, **13**. Whilst annoying, you can work round these defects. The more frustrating ones are those that only show up after the wood has been worked and finished. Bowls may warp or crack and the force is such that it can even crack inserts of marble or tile, **14**.

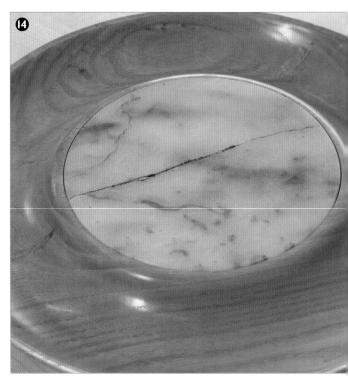

Never underestimate the strength of these drying stresses and remember that they are always the result of inadequate or faulty drying methods.

One method of ensuring complete dimensional stability was developed initially by gun-stock makers, but has since been much used by woodturners. The process relies on replacing the water within the wood with PEG (polyethylene glycol), a substance which is completely impervious to changes in atmospheric conditions and therefore renders the wood inert. Although quite feasible for the small-scale user, it is a rather messy process and the raw material is expensive. You need to cut and turn your blanks out of very fresh-sawn timber, as partly dry material is no use. The rough-turned blanks are then soaked in a vat of the warm PEG solution, often for several weeks, **⓯**. After a thorough soaking they can be force-dried and then finish-turned in the conventional way.

On a commercial scale, timber has to be treated in much the same way, but the logs are broken down on a bandmill, **⓰**. This works on the same principle as your home bandsaw but has a blade of up to 12in (305mm) wide, to deal with the logs, which are somewhat larger, **⓱**. The resulting boards are stacked outside to start the drying process, **⓲**, and may be left as whole trees with waney edges, or resawn with square edges, depending on the final application. Really thick material will take several years to air-dry outside and this time span is always reflected in the increased premium you have to pay when buying thicker-section blanks.

Kiln-dried timber

There is not time to air-dry most basic timbers, so the process is speeded up by kilning. Kiln-dried timber is ready for immediate use and sold with a specified moisture content, so you are reasonably sure that it will be stable. The drying kilns are like huge ovens, **⓳**, but with both the temperature and humidity closely controlled by highly sophisticated monitoring equipment, **⓴**. The contents can be dried in days or weeks rather than months or years, the exact timescale depending on species, thickness and initial moisture content.

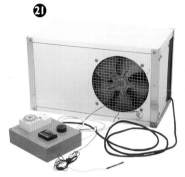

If you use a lot of timber you can actually build your own kiln for bulk drying. Although on a smaller scale than commercial kilns, these home units can turn out some very acceptable results. They work on the dehumidifying principle, with a small drying unit, **21**, being placed in an enclosed chamber with the stack of timber. You can either build the kiln from scratch, or convert something like an old refrigerator lorry body, **22**. They are well worth the relatively modest investment if you are a serious turner and have both the space and access to plenty of fresh timber.

Exotic timber

Many of the home-grown timbers are relatively bland and colourless; it is only when you get into the exotics that the highly decorative and colourful species appear, **23**. Notoriously expensive, these imported exotics are often only available in small sizes, primarily due to the quality of the logs. Even 'good' logs of species like African blackwood and tulipwood will be full of rot and shakes, making conversion into dimensions extremely wasteful, **24**.

Many of the species are effectively scrub trees and large sizes are rare, but some exotics do grow into big straight trees. Species like padauk, ovankol and purpleheart are available in large dimensions, but such logs often have huge bands of contrasting lighter sapwood which may or may not be considered a decorative feature, **25**. In home-grown timbers like yew, you can use the light sapwood to good effect, but it is amazing how this varies in both shape and quantity from tree to tree, **26**.

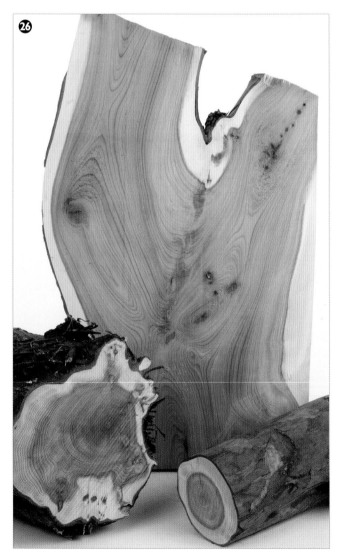

Look out for other features that will provide unusual timber suitable for turning. Branches joining the main trunk of a tree provide crotch figure where the normal growth structure becomes more convoluted, or a series of small branches create burr-like figure, **27**. Turning timber from this area provides wonderfully rich and varied patterns, though it is sometimes a little more difficult to work. Also look out for partially rotted or spalted timber, which can be quite magnificent when turned, **28**.

There is so much to learn about wood that you will never get to know it all. The material itself is diverse and variable, but as a woodturner you can learn to use virtually any piece of timber, even tiny offcuts for items like pens and light pulls, **29**. The skill is in using form and shape to exploit and enhance the natural characteristics. The fun is not only in the turning but also in the hunt for that special piece that you can later bring to life on the lathe, **30** and **31**.

Projects

Tool Handle

**Customizing your turning tools by making your own handles
is one of the simple projects and requires the bare minimum of tools.**

As a woodturner you have no excuse for not buying your tools unhandled and then turning your own! In reality there is often not much difference in cost, as the handle represents a very minor part of the expense. However, making your own does allow you to customize them to a shape that suits you, and also to code them in some way with different shapes or timber species to make them more instantly recognizable under the piles of shavings. There is also a quiet satisfaction to be gained from using a tool with a handle that you have fashioned yourself; somehow it always feels more personable as well as being more comfortable.

I have quite large hands and always find the standard handles are too small in diameter anyway, so tend to make mine slightly bulkier in section.

You need to work carefully; the handle should be with you for the rest of your turning career, so get it right. You can use any species of timber; traditionally turning tool handles are made of beech or ash, but more exotic species such as rosewood or box are sometimes used. The brass ferrules are available from most woodturners' suppliers, but if you are on a tight budget use offcuts of copper pipe – plumbers are usually happy to give away any very short pieces.

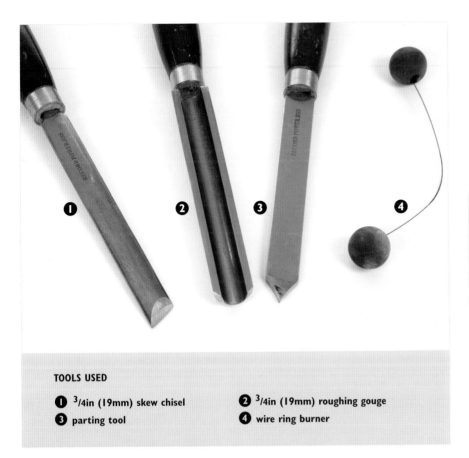

TOOLS USED

❶ ³/4in (19mm) skew chisel   **❷** ³/4in (19mm) roughing gouge

❸ parting tool   **❹** wire ring burner

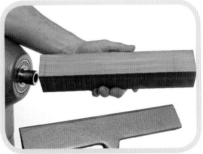

Select a suitable blank for the size of handle that you want. I used a piece of ash 12 x 2 x 2in (305 x 51 x 51mm) for the handle profile I prefer. You don't need to allow much for wastage, just ¹/2in (13mm) or so on the length.

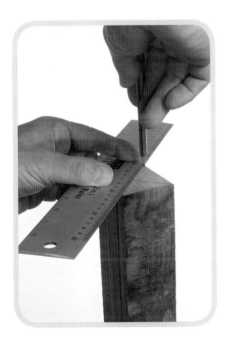

Find the centre of each end by drawing in the diagonals with a rule, or use a centre finder.

TIP: Pick out the centre point with a bradawl as a starter for the point of the drive centre. This helps the drive centre to penetrate, and stops it moving off line when you knock it in.

Use a wooden or soft-faced mallet to knock the centre into the blank. It doesn't need to penetrate far, but the wings must penetrate about ¹/20in (about 2mm). Don't use a metal hammer or you will burr over the end of the centre.

4 Ideally, use a revolving centre in the tailstock to reduce the risk of burning if you over-tighten. If you only have a dead centre apply a little wax as a lubricant, or it will scorch.

5 With the blank mounted between centres, check everything is tight and then spin the lathe by hand to make sure the toolrest is clear.

6 Use the roughing gouge to remove the corners, presenting the tool with the handle down and the tool angled to the right and also rolled slightly on its side.

7 With the lathe spinning at about 1500 rpm start working from left to right, working off the end of the blank, never onto it, or you might split off a complete corner which could fly off at you.

8 Keep working a bit further to the left with each cut, using your finger rubbing along the bottom of the toolrest as a guide to help you get a parallel cylinder.

9 When you get towards the left-hand end, stop the lathe and move the rest sideways. Never move the rest with the lathe spinning when there are still corners on the blank.

10 Now work off the end of the blank again, so move the tool from right to left for this section.

11 Use the finger-along-the-rest technique to make sure the two cuts end up meeting in the middle.

12 As the corners are removed, a wide gap opens up between the rest and the work. You can move the toolrest in closer without stopping the lathe, if you want. Increase the lathe speed to about 2000 rpm.

13 Mark off the length of the ferrule allowing approx. ⁵⁄₆₄in (2mm) of extra, to be trimmed off when the ferrule is in place.

14 Use a pair of callipers to reduce the diameter to just a fraction over the inside diameter of the ferrule.

15 To get the final fit using the ferrule itself as a gauge, fit it over your tailstock centre. If the centre is too big, temporarily replace it with a smaller dead one.

16 Now reduce the diameter with the parting tool, until the ferrule just slips on.

17 Don't worry about getting it tight, it just needs to be a sliding fit as any sloppiness will be lost later as you knock the tool tang in. However, if you make it too tight, the ferrule may split.

18 Once it is fitted tight up against the shoulder, slice off any excess length with the skew chisel on edge.

19 Now turn your attention to the headstock end and turn down a small waste spigot the same diameter as the drive centre.

20 The bulk of the shaping can be carried out with the roughing gouge, using it well on its side to get a nice clean slicing cut.

21 Fine tune the shape using the skew chisel to make a planing cut, radiusing down the tailstock end to meet the ferrule.

22 Repeat the procedure at the headstock end, rolling round the radius with the skew chisel and reducing the drive spigot diameter by about half.

23 Traditionally handles are decorated with incised lines. If you want to do this, use the skew on its side again to incise in from either side of the 'V'. Make the lines fairly deep at this stage, as the handle is yet to be sanded and they will then lose some depth.

CAUTION: I like to highlight the lines by burning them with a thin wire. Don't wrap the wire round your fingers when you do this, or the heat will travel back and burn you. Fit proper handles on either end of the wire.

24 Now sand the handle thoroughly, working down the grades of paper to 400 grit. Finish off by rubbing along the length of the grain with the lathe stopped.

25 I use three or four coats of cellulose as a finish, flatting back each coat with fine abrasive, then burnishing with wire wool and pastewax.

26 The finished handle is now ready for drilling. Note that the waste drive spigot is still in place at this stage.

27 Drill a hole fractionally less than the tang size, using a combination of drill sizes if the tang is tapered. For accuracy, I always start the hole with an engineer's centre drill, but this is not strictly necessary.

28 Fit the drill in a chuck in the headstock and wind the handle onto it with the tailstock, starting with the smallest diameter drill you are going to use.

29 Repeat this step using the next largest diameter drill bit, keeping a firm grip on the handle to stop it spinning.

30 Use the skew to slice down and separate the driving spigot waste. You should be able to cut down from either side until the handle is parted off with a clean end.

31 If you are not confident using the skew for this, use the parting tool to cut right through, catching the handle as it falls free. The small unpolished area can be sanded and finished off by hand.

32 Fit the tool in the handle; push it in as far as it will go and then bang the handle vertically down onto a block of softwood on a hard surface. If you have drilled the right-sized holes, it should gradually work its way in, hopefully without splitting the timber or the ferrule.

33 The finished made-to-measure tool, ready to go!

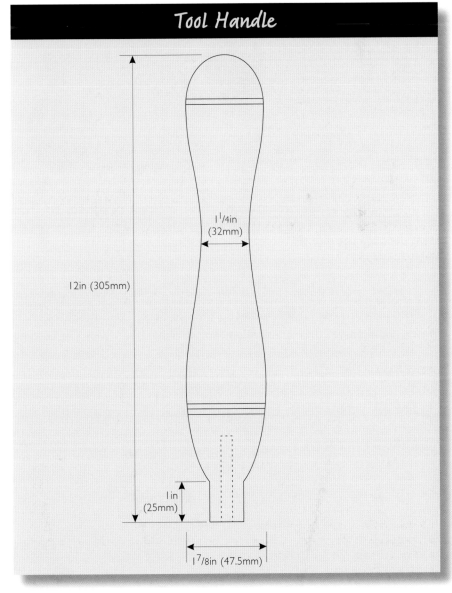

Tool Handle

1¼in (32mm)

12in (305mm)

1in (25mm)

1⁷/8in (47.5mm)

Light Pulls

Light pulls are one of the quickest projects to make and always sell well.

Light pulls are the ultimate project for using up all those odds and ends of scrap timber that are too small for anything else. However, I do sometimes wonder where all the light pulls go, as I am just one of thousands of woodturners who churn these out in vast numbers, yet they still continue to sell like hot cakes! A basketful of relatively low-priced light pulls on your stall at a craft fair will give you a good chance of making a few impulse-buy sales.

The design possibilities are limitless, ranging from very plain to highly ornate, but don't make them too big and heavy.

The ideal initial blank size is about 1 1/4in (32mm) square and 2 3/8in (60mm) in length. The more decorative exotic species usually sell first, but there is a good demand for more mundane species from those people with fitted kitchens, or bedrooms in oak or maple.

The turning process is very simple and, once the blanks have been drilled, you can knock them out in minutes, which makes them a good demonstration piece. You won't need many tools either, in fact you could probably do it all with just a 3/8in (10mm) spindle gouge, but I am going to show you various other options anyway.

TOOLS USED

❶ ³/4in (19mm) skew chisel   ❷ ³/8in (10mm) spindle gouge

❸ parting tool   ❹ ³/4in (19mm) roughing gouge

❺ light pull drive

If you are preparing blanks it is probably easiest to cut a whole batch while the bandsaw is set up for the correct size. Sort through all those offcuts and cut them down to size, even if you don't plan to use them straight away.

TIP: You can buy all sorts of specialized light-pull drives, many of which are far too elaborate and really quite expensive. You might be able to justify the cost if you anticipate making a lot of light pulls but, if your aims are more modest, you could make your own (see below)

2   **I have always made my own drives. Although these are to a large extent consumable, one should serve you well for several hundred pulls, and then it's only a few minutes to make another.**

3   **Turn the drive with a taper to match the internal Morse taper of your lathe headstock. If you use a fairly soft hardwood, this taper is not too critical, but get it as near perfect as you can by using a vernier to measure the correct diameters.**

4 The blanks need to be drilled at two different diameters. Ideally use a drill press and hold the blank in a drill vice, initially drilling the larger $^7/_{16}$in (8mm) hole to a depth of about $^3/_4$in (19mm).

5 Follow this up by drilling the smaller, $^5/_{64}$in (2mm) cord hole, right through the length of the blank. Keep withdrawing the drill to clear the swarf, or the flutes will clog and the hole will end up going off centre.

6 Aim to produce a blank with an internal section like the one shown above. The fine hole is to take the cord and the bigger one to hide the knot.

7 The first time you use your homemade drive, turn down the end to a spigot that is a tight fit in the knot hole of the blank.

8 Now you can mount the blank and bring up the tailstock to provide enough pressure to stop the blank spinning on the drive. If it does ever start spinning, apply a little water to the drive spigot to swell it and increase the grip.

9 Use the roughing-out gouge to knock off the corners. For these small blanks you can spin the lathe at about 2750 rpm, so the roughing process only takes a few seconds.

10 On a normal piece of spindle turning you would work off either end of the blank, turning the gouge round for each cut, but in this case it is quite safe – and much quicker – to work just the one way.

11 Rest your finger over the back of the blank as you hold the gouge, so you can tell when all the flats have been removed and the blank is truly cylindrical. Very light pressure is all you need on the gouge, or you will spin the blank on the drive spigot.

12 You should be able to complete virtually all the detail using the 3/8in (10mm) spindle gouge, but for better access I use one ground with a much longer bevel than normal.

13 This gouge can be used for virtually all the shaping work, by rolling it over onto its side from a flat position to form convex radiused shapes, and raising the handle as you roll to maintain bevel contact and ensure a fine cut.

14 Work the other way to form concave shapes, rolling the gouge from its side down onto its back as the cut progresses, again raising the handle as you go.

15 The very long bevel should allow you to work right up to the centre, but tighten up the tailstock to maintain the drive if you take any amount of timber away.

16 An alternative way of forming the tiny beads is to use the parting tool as a miniature skew chisel, rolling it over so the cutting edge becomes more or less vertical, but be careful not to catch the top, unsupported edge.

17 Similarly, you can use the skew for cleaning up the ends, the beauty of the wooden drive being that you can cut right through onto it without damaging the chisel.

18 Sand carefully with very fine abrasive, but don't spoil any of the nice sharp detail by overdoing it.

19 Light pulls need a really durable finish, as they have to stand up to a lot of handling. Start by rubbing in several coats of cellulose sanding sealer.

20 Flat these down with the finest abrasive you use and then burnish off the final one with some 0000 wire wool.

21 The top coat will be applied from an aerosol, so protect the lathe bed and tailstock to avoid covering them; I have a piece of cardboard for this purpose, that just wedges in place.

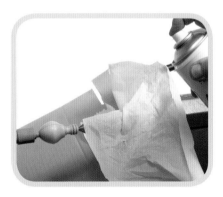

22 Acrylic-based spray lacquers are available in matt, satin and gloss. Use whichever you prefer, but these smaller items do look good with a high gloss. A quick spray and the job is done, but leave it to dry for five minutes or so.

TIP: More exotic timbers with a lot of figuring are best left as plain as possible, but make them a nicely rounded shape for comfortable gripping.

23 Plainer woods can be turned with more detail, or decorated in some way, such as wire burning. If you want to try this, start by incising a couple of lines with the top corner of the skew chisel.

24 Use a wire-burning tool to blacken the lines, but never wrap the wire round your fingers. For safety, fit proper handles on either end, as it gets very hot.

25 Wire burning needs to be applied with care, so don't overdo it, either in number of lines or amount of blackness. If you are not careful it can look like a tool handle, but applied sparingly it can liven up even the plainest of pieces.

26 Home-grown decorative species such as yew are wonderful for light pulls, particularly if they have some pin knots and purple colouration. Once again, don't put in too much detail, but use smooth, flowing shapes to highlight the figure.

TIP: After some use the spigot on the homemade light-pull drive will eventually wear smooth and the blank will start slipping and spinning. Soaking it with water will swell it enough to keep it working for a bit longer.

27 However, there will come a time when it won't grip any more, so just cut it away and form another one in its place.

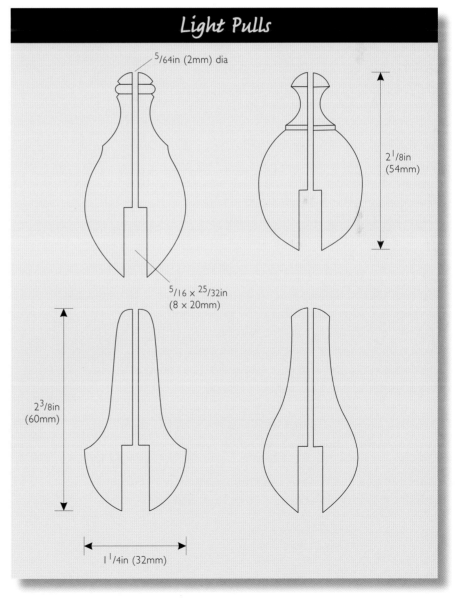

Light Pulls

5/64in (2mm) dia

2 1/8in (54mm)

5/16 × 25/32in (8 × 20mm)

2 3/8in (60mm)

1 1/4in (32mm)

Bird Box

Hollow out and shape an otherwise useless wet log to provide an elegant birdie starter home.

Woodturners often find large, wet logs difficult to deal with, because they are not really big enough to cut into planks but are usually too big to dry and use in the round. They are, however, perfect for a project like this bird box, where the moisture content is not important, and any cracking or warping just adds to the rustic charm of the finished project. Bird boxes are quick and fun to make and provide hours of entertainment as you watch the comings and goings of the various tenants.

Wet timber turns easily, pouring off the gouge in long streamers. However, it is important to ensure that you dry your tools and the lathe thoroughly when you have finished, or they will quickly rust. Oak and chestnut are particularly bad for this: the tannin in the wet sap is highly corrosive and will blacken the tools within minutes. I used oak for this one and, although it is a durable timber, the sapwood soon rots away and it is only the heartwood that will withstand being outside. Consequently, you will initially need quite large-diameter logs and to turn them down to remove as much sapwood as possible, using only the inner core of heartwood.

I did not sand or finish the timber in any way. Most hardwood timbers that are exposed to the weather soon turn an attractive grey colour and will withstand the elements without further treatment, for several years anyway. However, if you do decide on some form of preservative treatment, make sure it is non-toxic and bird friendly.

I have made several of these boxes over the years and have always found that it takes some time for them to find tenants. I think they need to acquire a weathered appearance before the birds feel comfortable. Try and place your bird box in a relatively sheltered spot to minimize the amount it swings about, then just sit back, wait and watch.

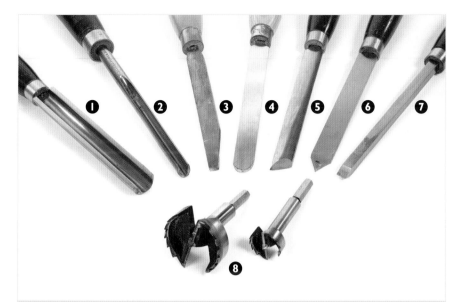

TOOLS USED

❶ ³/4in (19mm) roughing gouge   ❷ ³/8in (10mm) bowl gouge

❸ Square-side cutting scraper   ❹ 1in (25mm) round-nosed scraper

❺ ³/4in (19mm) skew chisel   ❻ standard parting tool

❼ ³/8in (10mm) parting tool   ❽ 2¹/2in (63mm) and ⁷/8in (22mm) sawtooth bits

3 Because of the unevenness, do take care with the initial positioning of the toolrest and swing the log round by hand to make sure it is well clear before you start up the lathe.

4 Depending on how uneven it is, spin the lathe at about 250 rpm to start with – until it all becomes balanced – and then increase the speed to what seems comfortable. I managed to turn this piece at 400 rpm, as it was naturally quite cylindrical, but each piece varies as regards the internal balance. If in doubt, start really slow and see what happens.

1 Use dividers or a compass to determine the maximum diameter of usable timber and mark the centre at either end. Offset this a bit if the log is badly bent or out of balance, although this can be corrected later as you will see.

2 Wet oak logs are heavy and uneven, so make sure the drive centre is well engaged by knocking it in deep with a mallet. A two-prong centre often penetrates better and provides a more positive drive for big pieces like this, though a four-prong centre will be fine provided the wings are sharp.

5 Start with the roughing gouge, nibbling away at the right-hand end to start with, then gradually working back further to the left with each successive cut.

6 With the slow revolution speed and irregularity of the blank, the initial roughing stages are usually quite slow, particularly if there is a large lump on one side. Take your time and present the gouge carefully, until you know exactly what you are dealing with. These lumps are not always clearly visible on the blank as it spins.

CAUTION: Because of the irregularity, always stop the lathe if you need to move the toolrest. Even at slow speed these large blanks have a fair bit of momentum, and will give you a nasty knock if you catch the toolrest.

7 Work from either end with the roughing out, it will become much easier as you gradually approach a true cylinder.

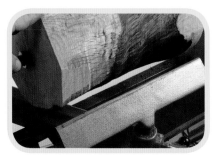

8 Large areas of bark often come loose as the roughing proceeds, so stop the lathe occasionally and remove any pieces that are likely to fly off at you.

9 As the irregularities are removed, a large gap will open up between the blank and the toolrest, so move it in as you work, to maintain maximum support for the tool.

10 You will soon be able to see if you didn't quite get the centring right, so reposition the centre position at one or both ends if necessary.

11 Use the parting tool to true up the ends, as this will remove a lot of the imbalance and vibration.

12 Once everything is running more smoothly, you can try increasing the speed a bit, to make the cutting process a lot easier. Go as fast as you can without making the lathe vibrate excessively, though this will depend on the internal balance of the blank.

13 Now you can quickly remove a lot of the outer sapwood and start the shaping at the top end. The roughing gouge will soon whip this away, which is great fun in wet timber.

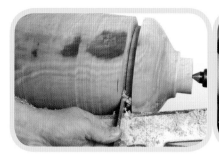

14 Form a long spigot on the top end of the blank, to fit the longest chuck jaws you have. Make sure the sides of the spigot are dead straight, as you need a really firm grip for these large sections.

15 Use the parting tool to mark where the join will be between the lid and the base, and form the internal flange on the underside of the lid.

16 To form the overhang of the lid, remove the bulk of the waste from the bottom end of the box, taking it down by about 3/8in (10mm).

TIP: When working with a wet log it is particularly important to seal it in a plastic bag if you have to leave it for any length of time. Even if it is just left overnight, part-turned work can split quite drastically without this sealing.

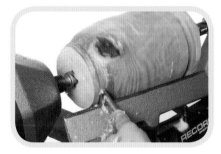

17 Next, shape the bottom end, swapping the roughing gouge for a 3/8in (10mm) bowl gouge as the radius gets tighter and the tool overhang increases. Complete the rough shaping of the outer profile, forming the overhang of the top.

18 Form another spigot on the bottom end, again making sure it is perfectly parallel. If you have one, a 3/8in (10mm) beading and parting tool is ideal for this heavy work.

19 Try and undercut the shoulder slightly, using the skew chisel as a flat scraper so that the blank seats squarely in the chuck.

20 Put in the internal flange that will form the join between top and bottom sections, making it about 3/8in (10mm) long. Then part through clear of this flange, going as deep as you can with the parting tool and widening the groove slightly as you go, to maintain some clearance for the tool.

TIP: When you are nearly through, stop the lathe and finish off with a handsaw, as it is so much safer than trying to part right through on these heavy sections.

21 Remount the top section in the spigot jaws, pushing the spigot shoulder tight up against the jaw surfaces to ensure that it is properly centralized.

22 Hollow out the inside of the lid to make the box lighter and to help minimize any splitting as it dries out. Leave the finish as it is straight off the gouge, as the birds will not appreciate you sanding it!

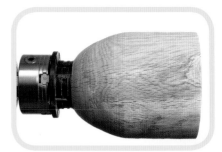

23 Remount the bottom end in a similar way. As long as your spigot is properly parallel and sized correctly, the chuck should be quite capable of holding a large blank like this. If you are having trouble maintaining a firm grip, check that the spigot is properly formed.

24 Use a drill in the tailstock to remove some of the centre waste and determine the maximum depth of hollowing. I find large sawtooth bits are the best for end-grain work, but keep withdrawing them to clear the swarf.

25 Start hollowing using a square-ended, side-cutting scraper, pulling it out from the middle towards the rim. Don't get too aggressive with this cut and keep the scraper angled downwards.

26 At this stage hollow out just deep enough to make the lid section a tight fit back in the base.

27 You can now use this base section as a jam chuck to turn the final profile of the top, my preference here being to use the 3/8in (10mm) bowl gouge.

28 The detail shouldn't be too complicated, because it needs to shed water easily, so form a gently sloping roof with a hanging knob at the top.

29 Take the lid off the base and finish off the internal hollowing, using a bowl gouge initially and then a heavy round-nosed scraper as the tool overhang starts increasing. Slacken the fit of the lid slightly, so that it takes on and off easily.

30 There are now options for re-chucking to complete the base turning: you can turn up a piece of scrap to act as a jam chuck for the base, leaving a long flange for maximum support, or you can use a set of Cole jaws, but remember that these don't have tremendous grip.

31 You can now complete the turning for the underside of the base, removing the tail-stock only for the final cuts.

32 Drill the entry hole through the side of the box using a saw-tooth bit. The exact size is critical, depending on the type of bird you want to attract. For small birds use a $1^{1}/8$in (28mm) drill, as anything larger will allow starlings and sparrows to enter.

33 Drill suitable pilot holes, then fix the base and lid back together with a couple of brass screws. The two sections will inevitably twist and warp as they dry out, but the screws will hold it together. Add a short length of hanging chain to complete the job.

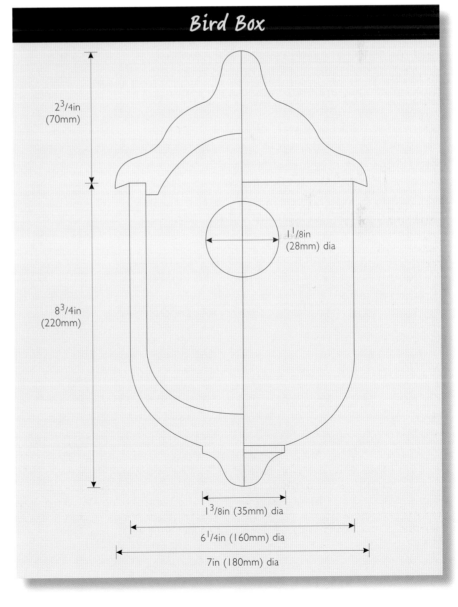

Bird Box

$2^{3}/4$in (70mm)

$1^{1}/8$in (28mm) dia

$8^{3}/4$in (220mm)

$1^{3}/8$in (35mm) dia

$6^{1}/4$in (160mm) dia

7in (180mm) dia

Candlestick

Make yourself this elegant holder and then bathe in the soft romantic glow of candlelight.

The modern trend of using candles seems to continue unabated and candlesticks of any form always make really acceptable gifts. They are also very popular at craft fairs, so consider turning a few for your next selling event. They can be big, small, fat or thin to match the huge range of candles that are currently available, making them an excellent way of using up some of those offcuts of timber that have been lurking under the bench for far too long!

This one-piece design is one of the simplest to make and you can amend the proportions to suit whatever timber you have available. Make it more detailed for the traditional look, or keep it really plain and simple for a more contemporary setting.

As candles come in a variety of shapes and sizes, you need to think about ways of holding them and the type of recess in the top of the candlestick. I have found that a $^7/8$in (22mm) hole suffices for most of the thinner styles, though I usually insert a standard tool ferrule to neaten up the hole. For bigger candles you can buy brass and steel cups that can be set into the end of the candlestick or even small saucers with a central spike to accommodate the very fat candles. All these accessories are available from the suppliers listed on page 168.

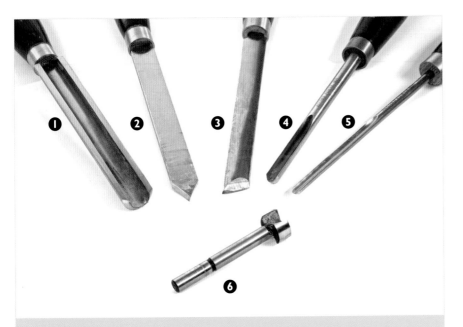

TOOLS USED

❶ ³/4in (19mm) roughing gouge   ❷ a parting tool
❸ ³/4in (19mm) skew chisel   ❹ ³/8in (10mm) spindle gouge
❺ ¹/4in (6mm) spindle gouge   ❻ ⁷/8in (22mm) sawtooth bit

2 Don't drill the hole too deep at this stage, or you will not be able to reach to the bottom with your tailstock centre; about ¹/2in (13mm) should be deep enough for now.

3 With a wooden mallet, knock in the headstock drive centre on the intersection of the diagonals, making sure that the wings engage fully in the timber.

1 Start by marking the centres at either end of the blank by drawing in the diagonals. Do this carefully if you want to maximize the biggest diameter you can get out of the blank. This yew blank is 3¹/4 x 3¹/4 x 7in (82 x 82 x 178mm).

TIP: For any piece of turning with a central hole it is essential to drill the hole first and then turn the profile with the blank centred on this hole. Turning the profile first and then trying to drill a concentric hole nearly always ends in failure, with the hole off centre. Use a drill press for maximum accuracy.

4 Mount the blank in the lathe, holding it between the centres by bringing the tailstock up into the pre-drilled hole.

5 Spin the blank a few times by hand to make sure that the toolrest is clear, and set the lathe speed to about 1000 rpm for the roughing-out stage on a blank of this size.

6 Use the roughing gouge with the handle well down, rolled on its side and angled slightly in the direction you're going to move it, i.e. left to right.

7 Start turning away at the corners at the right-hand end of the blank. Present the tool quite tentatively at first, as you cannot always see the corners when they are revolving at speed.

8 Keep working back a little further to the left with each successive cut, maintaining the same tool angle to make sure the bevel rubs and the top corners of the gouge remain clear of the work.

9 When you get near to the left-hand end, reverse the gouge position and then work from right to left, again with the handle of the gouge well down.

10 Keep reducing the whole length of the cylinder until there are no flat areas left. Practise holding the gouge and running your finger along the tool-rest as a guide, to get the cylinder as parallel as possible.

11 Use the parting tool to true up the top end and take just enough off to square it up. Present the tool with the handle well down to start with, then gradually raise the handle as the cut nears the centre.

12 Repeat the procedure at the bottom end, but this time angle the parting tool slightly inwards to form a hollow undercut on the base, so the finished candlestick will sit firm.

13 Use the parting tool again to mark in where each change of detail will be, making the cut down to somewhere near the finished diameter to give you a guide to work to with the shaping.

14 Most of the detail can be formed using the 3/8in (10mm) spindle gouge, keeping it well on its side with the bevel rubbing and always working downhill.

15 Don't be afraid to take away plenty of timber and make cuts over a wide area of detail, so you can see how the overall proportions develop.

16 Finer detail will need a 1/4in (6mm) spindle gouge, but use this in exactly the same way, rolling it down the sides on either side of the cove.

17 Beginners tend to make coves far too shallow and more 'V' shaped than 'U' shaped.

18 See how this looks much more elegant, with the sides steeper and the bottom of the candlestick more evenly rounded.

19 The main shaping of the stem is carried out very quickly and easily using the roughing gouge. I find a larger tool like this is easier to control on big areas than a spindle gouge.

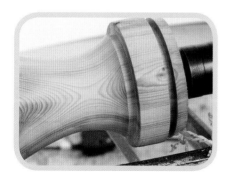

20 If you hold the gouge as I have shown, to keep the bevel in contact, the resulting finish should be really smooth with very little tearing, even on the end-grain areas.

21 Shaping a top end is another job for the 3/8in (10mm) spindle gouge, working down as close as possible to the revolving centre.

22 When access becomes too awkward because of the centre, finish off with a few slicing cuts using the skew chisel to leave a polished surface. (This is why it is important not to drill the candle hole too deep to start with.)

23 Use a skew chisel on its back to incise a tiny line at each definite change. This will sharpen up the appearance of the detail and make an amazing difference.

TIP: Reduce the speed to about 750 rpm for sanding. You risk overheating the surface and generating heat cracks in fine-grained timber like this if you spin the work too fast.

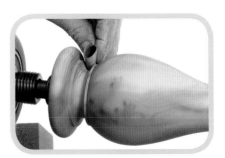

24 Sand carefully to avoid spoiling the detail; fold the abrasive into rolls and flats to get into all the nooks and crannies. Start at about 240 grit and then work progressively up the grades to 400 or 600.

25 Start the finishing process by applying two or three coats of cellulose sanding sealer, flatting down each coat when dry with the finest abrasive paper you used previously.

26 Burnish the final coat with 0000 grade wire wool to remove any excess sealer and to leave a perfect, smooth surface for polishing.

27 Apply a coat of pastewax with the lathe spinning. Allow it to dry for about an hour, then buff with a soft cloth.

29 If you are going to use an inserted ferrule, tap it in gently, using a rubber mallet to avoid damaging the edges.

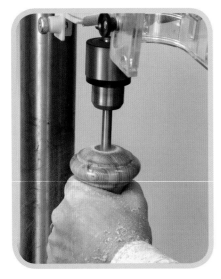

28 Remove the candlestick from the lathe and re-drill the hole deep enough to accommodate a standard candle, normally about 1in (25mm) in depth.

30 Grip a small piece of scrap timber in the combination chuck, then turn it to a very slight taper that will fit in the candle hole.

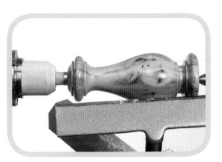

31 Use this as the drive and remount the candlestick in the lathe; bring the revolving centre up to engage in the centre mark left by the 4-prong drive.

32 Finish off the undercut of the base using the parting tool, cutting down as close as possible to the point of the revolving centre.

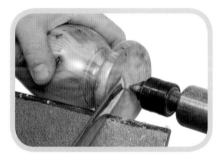

33 Give the candlestick a final polish and then, with the lathe stopped, slice off the tiny nib that is left using a skew chisel and turning the lathe by hand.

34 The finished candlestick should now sit firm and ready for action.

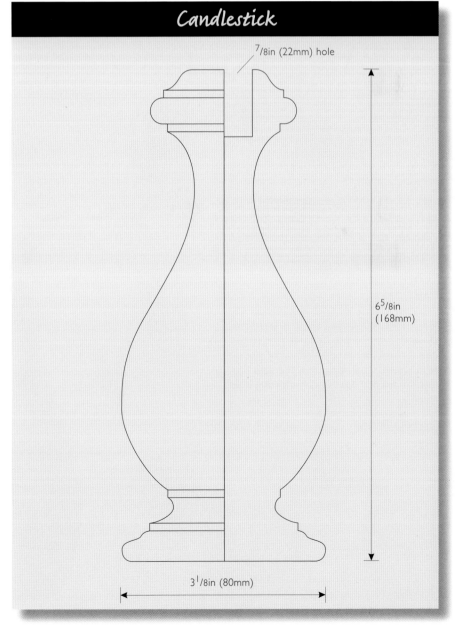

Candlestick

^{7}/8in (22mm) hole

6^5/8in (168mm)

3^1/8in (80mm)

Table Lamp

Shed a little light in a gloomy corner and highlight some beautiful timber with this elegant one-piece table lamp.

Table lamps are always good projects to make, as they are relatively simple to turn and yet you quickly end up with a useful and attractive item. The only slight difficulty is drilling down the centre to take the flex. However, as you will see, this is easily achieved with an inexpensive long-hole boring kit, and I'll give you a couple of tips for using the counterbore tool as well.

Depending on what material you have available there are two basic designs: you can either make it from two separate pieces with a thin-section spindle joined onto a separately turned larger-diameter base or, as in this case, from a single, large-section blank.

If you can find a blank with some really decorative figuring or colour it is often better to keep any fussy detail in the design to a minimum, leaving the wood to 'do the talking'. However, If your blank is relatively plain try putting in some nice beads and coves to make it more decorative, but always remember that with timber 'less is usually more' and don't overdo it.

CAUTION: If you are making lamps for sale, you now have to comply with certain CE regulations. Whilst you can self-certificate, there still appears to be some confusion about the exact interpretation of the regulations, depending on where you live. If you have any doubts, consult your local trading standards office for their view.

If you are not confident about the wiring procedure, always consult a qualified electrician.

TOOLS USED

1. ³/₄in (19mm) roughing gouge
2. ³/₄in (19mm) skew chisel
3. ³/₈in (10mm) spindle gouge
4. parting tool
5. long-hole boring kit

3 Set the bandsaw table to 45° and cut off each corner back to the scribed diameter line.

4 The cut-off corners are useful offcuts that can be used for small projects like pen making, or burnt, rather than having bags of useless shavings.

1 For this particular design I started with a square blank of ash 10 x 5 x 5in (254 x 127 x 127mm) and drew in the diagonals to find the centre at each end.

2 To save time turning and also minimize the amount of waste, I prefer to remove the corners of these large section blanks on the bandsaw, so use a compass to scribe the maximum available diameter.

5 Use a wooden mallet to knock in the drive centre, making sure all four wings are fully engaged in the timber.

6 Mount the blank between centres and spin it a few times by hand to make sure everything is clear of the toolrest. Set the lathe to its lowest speed to start with, until you see how the blank is balanced.

7 Use the ³/₄in (19mm) roughing gouge to true up the outside; starting at the right-hand end taking each successive cut slightly further to the left each time. Don't be too greedy with these initial roughing cuts as there will be a lot of unevenness in the early stages.

8 With the corners removed, there shouldn't be much work to do to get it fully round, but practise using your finger running along the toolrest as a guide to end up with a parallel cylinder. Increase the speed a little as the work becomes more and more balanced.

9 Always work off the end of the blank; as you approach the left-hand end turn the roughing gouge round and now work from right to left, keeping the handle down to maintain the bevel contact.

TIP: The blank needs to be bored for the lamp flex and it is far better to do it at this stage rather than after the detail has been turned, just in case anything goes wrong. Swap the revolving tailstock centre for a suitable hollow version.

10 Reduce the speed of the lathe to about 400 rpm and start boring using the long auger, feeding it in about 1in (25mm) at a time and then withdraw it to clear the swarf.

11 Once you have drilled about halfway, reverse the blank on the lathe, and replace the standard 4-prong drive centre with a counterbore tool having a ⁵/₁₆in (8mm) pilot, so that you can relocate the bored end accurately.

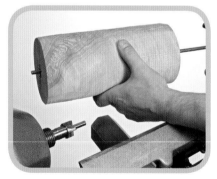

12 Repeat the drilling procedure from the other end and the two holes should meet perfectly in the middle. Most problems with this long-hole boring process are caused by forcing the auger too far for each cut and then not withdrawing it often enough to clear the build-up of swarf.

13 Now you can remount the blank using the standard revolving tailstock centre and increase the speed to what seems comfortable. A blank this size should turn at about 1200 rpm when properly balanced.

14 Start the initial shaping using the ³/₄in (19mm) roughing-out gouge again, which should quickly remove the bulk of the waste.

15 Trim up the base with a parting tool. Undercut it very slightly, so that the finished lamp will sit firmly without rocking.

16 Trim down as close as possible to the counterbore tool. Don't worry about the little stub that this leaves at this stage, it will be drilled away shortly.

TIP: You can continue the profiling using the roughing gouge, but now keep it quite flat – rather than rolled on its side – to increase the depth of cut to a fast and quite aggressive one. Use your hand as a shield to deflect the stream of shavings away from your face.

17 Finer detail can be put in with the ³/₈in (10mm) spindle gouge, but don't worry about getting too close to the revolving centre at the top end, as this will also be drilled away later on.

18 Continue refining the detail as the proportions change. I find the best tool for the long sweeping curves is still the roughing gouge, but give it a quick sharpen up for the final cuts.

19 Finalize the top detail again, keeping any curves flowing smoothly and, working with the spindle gouge, cut any coves down from either side, into the bottom.

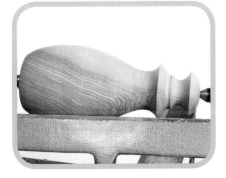

20 The finished profile with a minimum amount of detail. The smooth flowing curves have been left to accentuate the distinctive brown colouration of this piece of olive ash.

21 Now stop the lathe and slacken off the tailstock centre. Pull the blank off the driving wings of the counterbore tool, leaving it supported just on the centre pilot.

22 Hold the blank firmly, start the lathe up again and then, using the tailstock, wind it onto the spinning counterbore tool, drilling in about 1in (25mm) in depth.

23 Decide which face of the lamp is going to be the back and then drill a $^5/_{16}$in (8mm) hole in from this face to meet the counterbored hole in the base.

24 Reverse the blank on the counterbore tool, and this time drill a $^1/_8$in (3mm) deep recess to take the lamp fixing plate.

25 The counterbore in the base allows the cable that comes in from the side hole to be bent round and up the main central hole.

26 Replace the blank in the lathe and trim off the tiny amount of excess left after the counterboring.

27 Carefully sand and polish the lamp, working down the grades of abrasive: start at 180 grit and finish at about 400 grit, or maybe 600 grit for a fine-textured timber.

28 Take care not to spoil the nicely contrasting, sharp detail by over-sanding. Use a small piece of abrasive carefully folded to get into any tight corners without rounding them over.

29 Polish the lamp with the finish of your choice. For these larger pieces I prefer to use about four coats of cellulose sanding sealer, thoroughly rubbed down between each coat, then polished with some soft pastewax.

30 If you have time, allow the pastewax to dry fully for about an hour before giving the lamp its final burnish with a soft cloth.

31 Fix the lamp-holder plate into the top recess, using three small brass screws.

32 The counterbored hole in the base allows the cable to bend round neatly from the side entry.

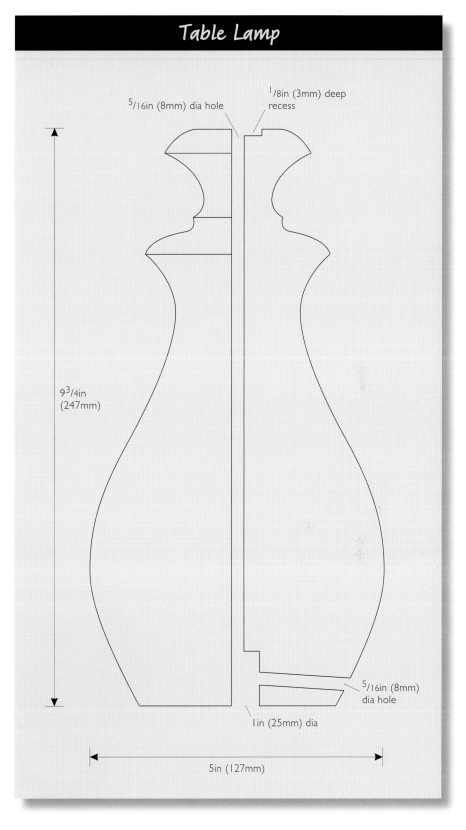

Table Lamp

^{5}/16in (8mm) dia hole

^{1}/8in (3mm) deep recess

9^3/4in (247mm)

^{5}/16in (8mm) dia hole

1in (25mm) dia

5in (127mm)

Finial Box

Everyone loves little boxes and they're very quick to make, so give one a try.

I really enjoy making little boxes like this. There are endless possibilities for both size and design and the finished results will always find a loving home. You can use virtually any type of timber, but the smaller ones in particular always look better if you can use something fine textured and really decorative. This tends to limit you to homegrown species like yew or box, or to the more expensive exotic timbers, so plan the design carefully to minimize any waste. I strongly believe that we have a responsibility to use these beautiful woods with care and to treasure their heritage.

For this box I used a piece of rosewood I have had in the workshop for a number of years. The block started out at 3 x 3 x 6in (76 x 76 x 152mm) and there was very little left over at the finish. I have found that the only snag with using rosewood, apart from the cost, is that the black powdery dust makes your hands really dirty, although it does eventually wash off.

Being a really hard timber, you can either cut it in the conventional way with gouges, or scrape it to shape without any risk of tearing the grain. In fact the scraping option sometimes leaves a better finish on these very hard timbers. Don't be afraid to experiment a little to find which tools work best for you.

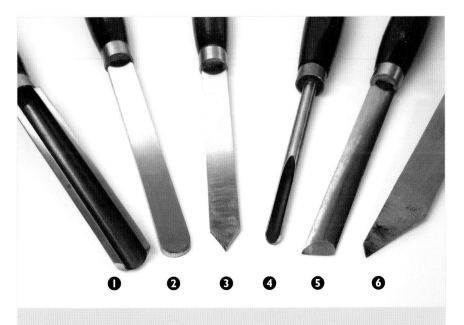

TOOLS USED

❶ ³/4in (19mm) roughing gouge   ❷ ³/4in (19mm) round-nosed scraper
❸ standard parting tool   ❹ ³/8in (10mm) spindle gouge
❺ ³/4in (19mm) skew chisel   ❻ thin section parting tool

With expensive exotic timber it is better to try and save every scrap, by cutting off the corners rather than turning them off. See what's going to be waste, by scribing in the maximum diameter circle on one end.

With the ends of the blank trimmed up square, first find the centre by drawing in the diagonals, or using a centre finder.

Set the bandsaw table to 45° and cut off each corner, running the blank against the rip fence to get all the cuts even.

Now you have four small, but useful offcuts ideal for pen or bobbin making, or for use as inlays, rather than a pile of useless shavings.

5 Mount the block between centres, although you may have to drill a small hole to accommodate the point of the drive centre and help the wings penetrate properly, if the timber is very hard.

6 Use the 3/4in (19mm) roughing gouge to turn up the true cylinder. This won't take long with the bulk of the corners already removed and you should be able to spin it at about 2000 rpm.

7 Hold the gouge between finger and thumb and slide your finger along the rest, using it as a guide to form a parallel cylinder.

8 Set a pair of callipers to a fraction bigger than the closed diameter of your chuck jaws – this is not critical but it should be somewhere near.

9 Use the parting tool to form a matching gripping spigot at this diameter on either end of the blank. Don't make it too long or the spigot will 'bottom' in the chuck, rather than sit firmly on the shoulder.

10 Use a skew chisel as a flat scraper to undercut the shoulder of this spigot slightly and also to form a slight inwards taper to it.

TIP: Decide where the join between lid and base will be and use a very narrow parting tool to start cutting through. This narrow tool is essential to minimize the amount of waste and therefore grain disruption when the two halves are fitted back together later. It may not be important with plain timbers, but the more decorative ones look so much better if the grain lines up through the base and top.

11 Even a narrow cut like should be widened a little as you go, to stop the tool binding and overheating. Just waggle it slightly as you feed it in, to generate some clearance.

12 Cut down to leave about 3/8in (10mm) diameter and then stop the lathe. I do not recommend parting right through when a piece is held between centres like this.

13 Complete the cut using a handsaw, backing off the tailstock centre slightly to stop the saw binding.

14 Start forming the outer profile of the base using the spindle gouge, rolling it over in the manner of a big bead. You should get an almost polished finish straight off the tool if the bevel is kept rubbing.

15 Follow the same procedure for the bottom end of the base section, but work carefully with the gouge and parting tool to avoid cutting too near to the chuck. I should really have left a bit more room here but didn't want to waste any timber!

16 Complete the initial hollowing of the inside with the spindle gouge, working down the curve from the rim to the centre. Drill out some of the waste if you want, but it is probably just as quick to turn it out on these small projects.

17 Eventually you will probably struggle to get the gouge round far enough inside to keep it cutting, so swap to a round-nosed scraper for the final shaping, using it tilted slightly on its side for a really clean, shearing cut.

18 With these small boxes the shavings get trapped inside and obscure your view of what is going on, leaving you to do a lot of the work by 'feel'. The only answer is to keep stopping the lathe and clearing the swarf.

19 Angle the top lip of the box inwards slightly, so that the lid will fit up tight. The best tool for this is the scraper, again tipping it on its side for a shear cut.

20 Remove the base section from the chuck, replace it with the top section and use the parting tool to form a small spigot that will be a tight fit in the base.

21 Take your time with this, as the two really must be a tight fit, but don't make it so tight that you split the box. Lots of trial and error, stopping the lathe and checking, is the only way to get it perfect.

22 Next, hollow out the underside of the lid to make it lighter; use either the gouge or scraper, but bear in mind the final shape you want on the top, so you don't take away too much.

23 Sand and polish the inside of the top, as you will not be able to access it again until the whole job is finished.

24 Put the base section back in the chuck, press the lid on and bring up the tailstock for a bit of additional support.

25 Shape the top section, allowing for the amount you hollowed away on the inside.

26 For the delicate top finishing cuts, rest your hand behind the spinning timber to add a bit of support. Complete the final profile, but leave a tiny nib for the tailstock centre to run in. If you are confident that the lid is held firmly, cut this nib away as well.

27 Sand the outer surface, using only very fine abrasive or you will scratch the surface of these hard exotics. I would normally finish at about 800 grit for a superfine finish.

TIP: Small decorative items like this are good candidates for a high-gloss finish, my preference being friction polish on top of several coats of cellulose sanding sealer. Use sealer and oil or pastewax if you don't want the finish to be quite so glossy.

28 With the polishing complete, carefully part off the final nib with a skew chisel and finish this tiny section to match the rest.

29 Remove the lid and just ease the fit of the lid a fraction by lightly sanding the inside of the base, then sand and polish the whole inside.

30 Turn a piece of scrap wood in the chuck with a spigot, so that it will be a tight fit in the base opening.

31 Push the base onto this spigot as a jam fit, pressing it tight up against the shoulder to make sure it runs true.

32 Carefully clean up the underside of the base using the gouge, either put in a bit of detail or leave it plain, then sand and polish to complete the job.

Finial Box

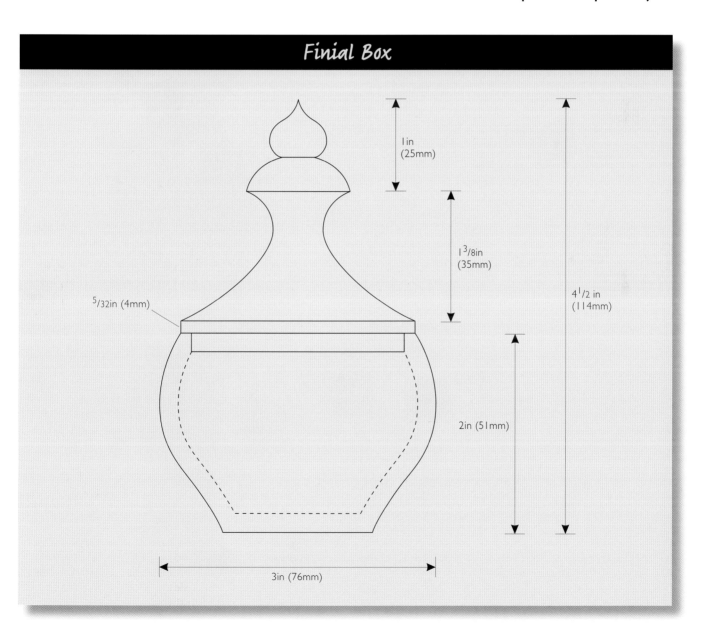

1in (25mm)

1³/8in (35mm)

⁵/32in (4mm)

4¹/2 in (114mm)

2in (51mm)

3in (76mm)

Table Leg

Master the art of turning pummels, that tricky bit where the square changes to round.

This table-leg project uses just five tools and addresses the often awkward problem of forming pummels, which is the technical term for the square section left on the top of a leg when the rest of it is turned.

Achieving clean and neat cut edges on these pummels is actually quite straightforward, provided you follow a few basic rules, and you can even experiment with a variety of different shapes in the transition area from square to round.

As these table legs are always made in multiples it is essential that the pummel area is clearly marked on each blank before you start, and that you then work progressively back to the line as shown in the sequence. Otherwise any discrepancies in the length of the pummels will be highlighted when you subsequently add the rails to make up the rest of the table frame.

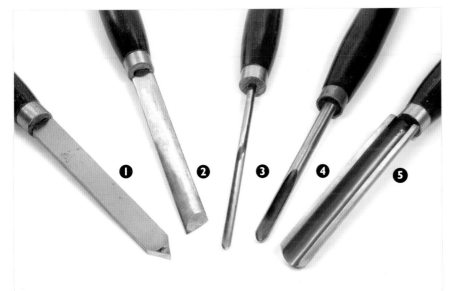

TOOLS USED

❶ parting tool

❷ ³/4in (19mm) skew chisel

❸ ¹/4in (6mm) spindle gouge

❹ ³/8in (10mm) spindle gouge

❺ ³/4in (19mm) roughing gouge

3 Mount the blank carefully on the lathe, making sure the centres remain in place and that the toolrest is adjusted to be clear of the spinning corners. For a 2¹/2in (63mm) section blank I would start the lathe at about 2000 rpm.

TIP: A quicker and more accurate method of centring at the headstock end is to use your chuck, but the jaws will usually then mark the surface – not a problem if you can leave the blank slightly over length and then trim off the excess, or plane it later to remove the marks.

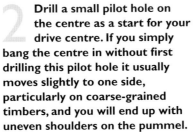

1 First, it is essential to mark out carefully. Draw on the blank where you want the pummel to be formed, marking the line clearly so that it can be seen as the lathe is revolving. Then mark the centre at each end; this must be spot on, or the pummel will be off-centre relative to the turned section. A dedicated centre finder makes this job relatively foolproof.

2 Drill a small pilot hole on the centre as a start for your drive centre. If you simply bang the centre in without first drilling this pilot hole it usually moves slightly to one side, particularly on coarse-grained timbers, and you will end up with uneven shoulders on the pummel.

4 First, use the skew chisel to make a slicing cut, separating the square area from the turned section. This cut must be made first, as it prevents the corners breaking off the pummel during the roughing-out process. A thin, oval-section tool makes this easier, but is not essential.

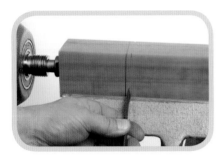

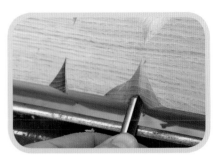

5 Use the skew with the long edge on the toolrest. Push it gently into the revolving timber to make the first incision in the waste area, some distance away from the marked line. Don't force the cut, or you will get ridges on the shoulders. If you do get ridges, angle the chisel slightly off the vertical, away from the square section; this reduces the vibration and can leave a smoother cut.

6 Take progressively deeper cuts in from either side, gradually working back to the line to form a nicely radiused shoulder on the pummel. Make sure you keep an eye on the presentation of the skew, to prevent the unsupported top edge from digging in. Keep it upright.

TIP: Alternatively, use the spindle gouge to produce a form of shaped entry to the pummels. The technique is very similar to that using the skew, but start with the gouge on its side and cut away from the pummel into the waste area. Experiment with different profiles in the waste area before you continue. An ogee shape is an attractive alternative to standard radiused ends on the pummel, but remember that more elaborate shapes are harder to reproduce if you have several matching legs to make.

8 Although the blank now looks truly round, there are often quite large flats remaining; these can be felt quite safely by gently resting your fingers on the back of the revolving workpiece, which saves continually stopping and starting the lathe to check. If you centred the work accurately at the start any flats should be even on all four faces.

7 With the pummel clearly delineated, the roughing-out gouge is used. Start the roughing-out process at the right-hand end; present the tool to the wood with the handle well down, the flute rolled slightly on its side and pointing in the direction of travel. Work the tool from left to right, coming back a little further to the left with each cut so you only remove a small section at a time and end up with a reasonably parallel cylinder.

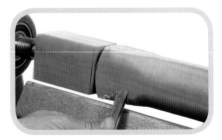

9 Be careful with the roughing-out process as you approach the pummel, turning the gouge over to remove the last section of the corners.

10 With a gouge that is ground square across, you can use the outer wing to clean right up to the shoulder, or you could use a parting tool if you are less confident with the gouge.

11 The first roughing-out stage is to produce a straight cylinder with the pummel on the end, hopefully with nice neat shoulders!

12 Next, use a parting tool to cut in to the required depth at the point of each detail change – this greatly helps the copying process if you have to make several the same.

13 Remove the initial waste, using the roughing gouge well on its side to reduce the width of cut.

14 The $3/8$in (10mm) spindle gouge is the main tool for the detail shaping, but always cut downhill for the concave surfaces.

15 For convex surfaces, start with the tool relatively flat on the top of the bead with the bevel rubbing, then gradually roll the tool over, swinging the handle in the same direction to maintain bevel contact around the curve. Take several light cuts to get the required radius rather than trying to do it in one heavy cut.

16 For larger areas of waste the roughing gouge can be used with a fair degree of precision and may actually be easier to control – find which tool suits you best for each particular situation.

17 Small or difficult-to-access beads are best cut with the skew chisel, slicing down from either side, again taking light cuts each time.

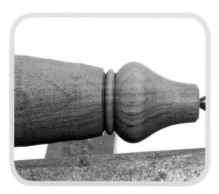

18 Whatever their size, beads should be even and smoothly radiused, rather than being too pointed.

19 Use the roughing gouge for the long slow curve of the main section of the legs. With the relatively short bevel of this tool the finish may be a series of very small ridges rather than a nice smooth surface …

20 … so finish off with the skew, taking light planing cuts but angling the tool so that the cutting edge is virtually square to the direction of travel, to ensure a very fine cut.

21 The coves are cut with a spindle gouge, although for delicate work you may find the standard $^3/_8$in (10mm) version too wide, as you risk catching the top unsupported edge.

22 If so, use a $^1/_4$in (6mm) version. Start with the tool on its side, then roll it onto its back as the cut proceeds down to the required depth. Make cuts from either side of the cove, working down-hill into the middle from either side, never down one side and up the other.

23 Use the same tool to roll over the beads, working the other way round this time, starting with the tool flat on its back and rolling it onto its side down the side of the bead.

24 Repeat the procedure for each successive bead, aiming to match those that are close together. Take plenty of material away from the cove, making the sides quite steep with a nicely radiused bottom. Beginners tend to make beads very shallow and uneven.

25 To sharpen up the profile, use the skew to incise a very shallow line at each change of detail.

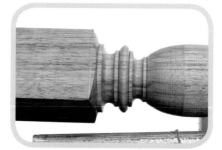

26 This will make an amazing difference to the finished appearance as everything will look much crisper.

27 Be very gentle with any sanding, folding the abrasive so that the sharp corners you have so carefully created are not rounded over by careless working, or a stray flap of abrasive.

28 If you use these proper cutting techniques the completed leg should only require a minimal amount of sanding, even on hard, open-grained timber like this oak.

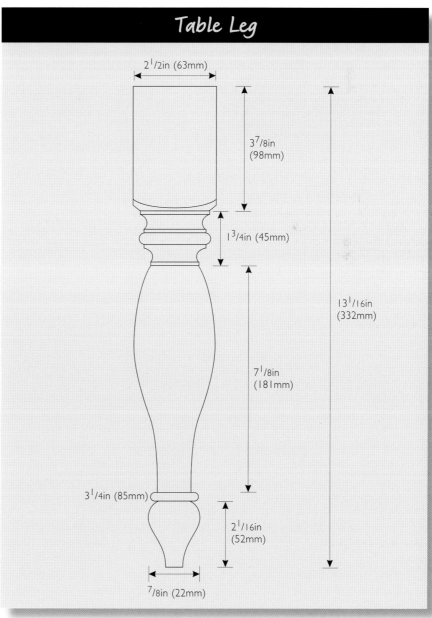

Table Leg

2¹/₂in (63mm)

3⁷/₈in (98mm)

1³/₄in (45mm)

13¹/₁₆in (332mm)

7¹/₈in (181mm)

3¹/₄in (85mm)

2¹/₁₆in (52mm)

⁷/₈in (22mm)

Cabriole Leg

Try some simple off-centre turning to produce this cabriole-style leg.

Although often described as a cabriole leg, the result of this off-centre turning is not strictly a cabriole leg, but rather the nearest approximation you can get using a conventional lathe. Proper cabriole legs are more highly shaped and involve a lot of cutting on the bandsaw and then even more handwork. Commercial cabriole legs are made on a copying lathe with variable centres and an array of fixed tooling to form the shape in one pass.

Whatever you want to call it, this type of leg is a common feature of stools and tables, adding a bit of style, even to a more contemporary design and, once you have got the hang of the principle, they are actually very quick to produce.

The technique is quite straightforward, with accurate marking being the key to success, but you do need to be careful with the turning during the off-centre phase, as it generates a lot of vibration and you cannot always see clearly what is happening at the cutting edge.

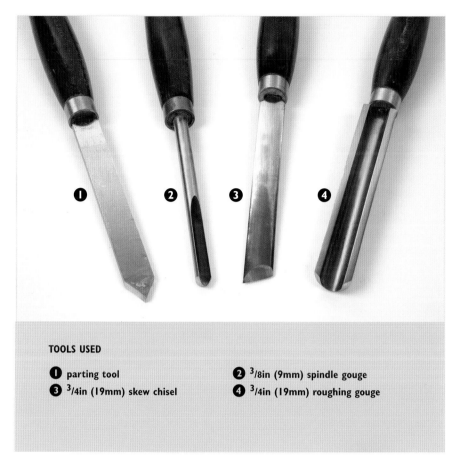

TOOLS USED

❶ parting tool

❸ ³/4in (19mm) skew chisel

❷ ³/8in (9mm) spindle gouge

❹ ³/4in (19mm) roughing gouge

3 Knock in the drive centre, making sure it stays in the centre pilot hole and that the wings are really well engaged.

Start by marking out clearly where the square pummel is to be, and machine any mortices at this stage, as it will be much more difficult to hold the leg for morticing after it has been turned.

2 Mark the centres by drawing in the diagonals, drilling a tiny pilot hole to help locate the centre accurately when you knock it in. The drive centres must be absolutely dead on when doing any work that involves leaving squares, or you end up with flats on the detail.

4 Mount the work between centres, checking that everything is secure and the toolrest is brought up as close as possible. The speed should be about 1500 rpm for a piece like this 2¹/2in (63mm) square blank, provided it is reasonably well balanced.

5 For once the first tool to use is the skew chisel, not the roughing gouge, and I prefer the thinner, oval-section type for this sort of work.

6 To separate the pummel, make an incision with a skew chisel resting on its back. Approaching the spinning work carefully, make the first cut well into the waste side of the pummel line.

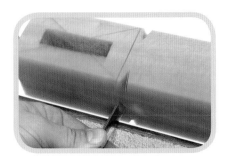

7 Gradually work back towards the line with each successive cut, making them a little bit deeper each time, until you eventually reach the line.

8 Only take very light cuts, otherwise the chisel will bounce around and you'll end up with a series of ridges on the pummel ends.

9 Finish off with a single light slicing cut all the way in, to leave a clean face to the pummel ends. A shallow bevel angle ground on the skew is also a great help here if you are struggling.

10 Once the pummel has been established, you can safely rough the rest of the blank down to a cylinder, but always stop the lathe before moving the toolrest, in case you catch the pummel corners.

11 Start roughing out from the right-hand end using the gouge with the handle well down to maintain bevel contact. The cut is very intermittent to start with, but you will soon get some bevel support.

12 Start each successive cut a bit further back to the left each time, cutting down until the cylinder is perfectly round with no flats remaining.

13 If you are confident enough you should be able to work up to the pummel shoulder with the gouge rolled right over on its side to cut with the outer wing.

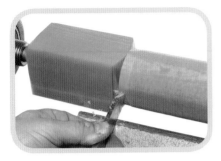

14 If you are not too happy doing this with the gouge, use the parting tool instead to cut a neat transition from square to round.

15 Once the corners have been removed, a big gap opens up between the rest and the wood, so move it in carefully to minimize the amount of tool overhang.

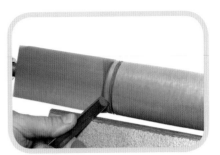

16 Complete any turned detail at the top of the leg, using the skew chisel on its back to get in tight against the shoulders.

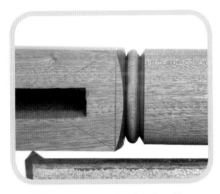

17 Don't overdo the detail, as it will end up slightly off centre when the leg centres are moved. However, this shouldn't show unless you come too far down the leg with it.

18 Next, determine the amount of offset for the foot. Usually, the narrow 'ankle' of the foot is half the diameter of the main cylinder, so you need to measure the diameter of the cylinder just below the square section.

19 Here, the diameter is $2^1/2$in (63mm). Divide this figure in half to give the ankle diameter, then divide it in half again to give the amount of offset necessary to achieve this. So $2^1/2$in (63mm) $\div 2 \div 2 = {}^5/8$in (15.75mm). For a stool or chair leg where the foot is to point out towards the corner, mark this offset out on the diagonal, measuring away from the centre.

TIP: Orientate it correctly relative to the mortices in the top of the leg, or the foot will point the wrong way (it should be on the diagonal that divides the two mortices). Remount the leg on this new centre, making sure it seats accurately.

20 On a long leg this is enough to provide an accurate offset, but on a shorter one offsetting just this one centre will result in the top being slightly eccentric as well. As you want the top part to remain true to the original centres, the trick is to move the top centre slightly in the opposite direction to the bottom one. This makes such a difference to the finished appearance. Determining exactly how much you offset the top is a matter of trial and error; keep making tiny adjustments until it runs more or less true again.

21 Before starting the lathe, spin the work by hand to check clearances – with this amount of eccentricity you do not want the work smashing into the toolrest. Check the toolrest for security as well, as the inevitable vibration will try and loosen it.

22 Set the speed down a notch or two as well to help minimize this vibration. In this case I have reduced it to 950 rpm to allow for the imbalance.

23 Start roughing out again, approaching the wood carefully as you cannot see the extremity very clearly. Aim to reduce the blank down to the diameter based on the new centres, which shows up as a solid ghost image within the blur of the revolving work.

24 There is very little contact with the tool when you start. This will increase progressively as you cut further in, but hold the tool firmly on the rest to stop it bouncing at the start of the cut.

25 As you scoop away the foot begins to form, but stop the lathe regularly to see how the shape is developing.

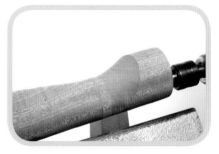

26 The blank will eventually appear cylindrical again, but there may be a flat left on the back of the leg. You will have to turn down further to get rid of it and achieve the correct ankle diameter.

27 I use a shallow 3/4in (19mm) roughing gouge for the whole operation. You can form the foot with this as well, as the size and bulk of the gouge provide extra support where the tool overhangs the rest to scoop in the foot. A smaller gouge is likely to vibrate too much with this amount of overhang.

28 When you are happy with the shape, stay on the 'off-centre' centres and sand the leg thoroughly, using the abrasive wrapped around a block for the straight sections.

29 Take care near the foot section. Hold the abrasive underneath the revolving work, gradually blending the straight and radiused sections together.

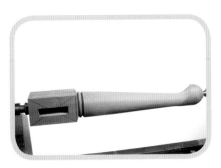

30 Now return the blank to the two original centres and shape the underside of the foot using a spindle gouge. You can make the toe as heavy as you want, simply by making the foot more bulbous.

31 Do any shaping work at the top of the leg as well, then finally sand these centres again, to blend the two profiles.

TIP: You might need to do a bit of final hand sanding with the lathe stationary to finish the transition area.

The finished leg. It is not a true cabriole, but it is the nearest you will get on a standard lathe.

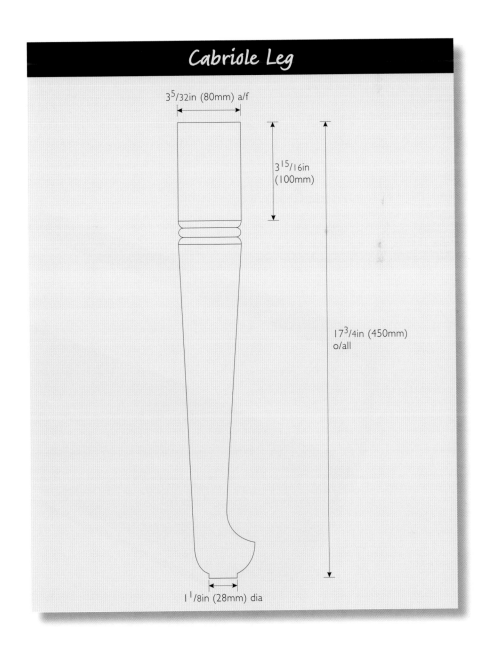

Cabriole Leg

$3^5/32$in (80mm) a/f

$3^{15}/16$in (100mm)

$17^3/4$in (450mm) o/all

$1^1/8$in (28mm) dia

Pen

There is something very satisfying about using hand-turned pens made from some exotic timber and they're so easy to make.

Pen making has become extremely popular, in fact there are turners who make nothing else, such is the market for unique, nicely made wooden pens. However, you are not restricted to just using wood; pens can be turned in a variety of other materials: offcuts of Corian worktops turn up nicely and there is a whole range of other plastic and acrylic materials specially made for pen making. Other turners laminate blanks up from coloured veneers, or use bone and horn.

The mechanisms are available in a huge variety of designs and qualities, and you can make pencils and fountain pens to match. The various suppliers can also kit you up with presentation sleeves or boxes for your finished pen to make it even more distinctive.

You must work very carefully to get the exact sizes and there is very little room for error but, if something does go wrong, not much material is lost. Pen blanks are obtainable ready-cut to size, but I tend to cut my own from offcuts and scraps salvaged from bigger blanks.

Any wood will turn into a pen, but the fine-grained and more decorative ones are best, as they will stand turning to the very thin sections required. However, the highly decorative burrs and curls are much more difficult to work, so save these until you have gained some experience.

I suggest starting with a simple parallel design, to get the hang of the procedure. Instructions are normally supplied with each pen, but the principles are the same for most designs.

With pen making more than any other type of turning, it is important to work methodically, as you are using a lot of very small components that are easily lost and need to be assembled in the right order. The most critical stage is the initial drilling and it is worth investing in a top-quality drill bit to ensure the hole is exact size and doesn't wander off along the length of the blank.

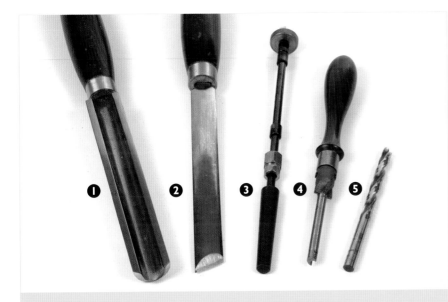

TOOLS USED

❶ ³/4in (19mm) roughing gouge   ❷ ³/4in (19mm) skew chisel

❸ mandrel   ❹ barrel trimmer

❺ ⁵/16in (8mm) drill bit

2 Now it is safe to cut the blanks through the middle, leaving them about ¹/8in (3mm) longer than the length of the brass barrels.

3 For these straight pens you will need a sharp ⁵/16in (8mm) bit – my preference is the brad type with a central spur.

If you are cutting the blanks yourself, make them slightly oversize, as the drill bit nearly always goes off line slightly. I cut mine about ⁹/16in (15mm) square if there is enough material.

TIP: Cut the blanks full length first, then draw a short line through the centre and mark them with an identification letter to help you keep the correct grain orientation throughout the making process. The pen will only look its best if this original grain continuity is maintained.

4 For accuracy, use a drill press with the blank held securely in a drill vice and drill from the middle outwards on each blank.

5 Drill slowly and carefully, allowing the swarf to clear. If you force the drill and the blank becomes too hot, it will crack when you turn it down to the final thin diameter.

6 No matter how carefully you set up the vice, the hole will always go a little off centre at the exit end, which is the reason it is necessary to cut the blanks slightly oversized.

7 If you don't have a drill press, use the lathe with the drill chuck fitted in the headstock and feed the blanks onto the drill with pressure from the tailstock. With this method, leave the blanks slightly over length and trim them afterwards, as you cannot drill right through without damaging the revolving centre.

8 The brass barrels must be a snug sliding fit in the hole – if they are loose it will be hard to turn the wood down thin without it breaking up. The drill bit has to be good quality and sharp to achieve this sort of accuracy.

9 Use superglue to stick the barrels in place. The very thin type will do, but a slightly thicker one, with a longer curing time, will allow you to get things lined up properly before it grabs.

10 Paint the glue onto the outside of the barrels, holding them on a screwdriver so that you don't get glue all over your hands.

11 Use the same arrangement to slide the barrel into the bore, making sure it goes well in. Act quickly, as the glue will soon grab hold of it if you hesitate too long.

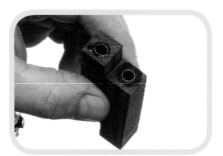

12 If you have cut the blanks to the right length to start with, the brass barrel should finish up just below the surface of the timber at both ends.

13 To trim them to exact length the ideal tool is a barrel trimmer, which will also clean out any stray glue that might have got into the inside of the barrel.

14 I prefer the hand-operated trimmers as they are more controllable, but they are available to fit in an electric drill. Take care if you do use one of these, as it is very easy to trim the barrel too short.

15 Trim the timber back until it is just flush with the end of the barrel, no further.

16 To hold the barrels for turning you will need a mandrel.
These either fit directly into the tailstock, or can be gripped in the drill chuck. There are various sizes to suit the size of pen you are making, but many of them use a $^5/16$in (8mm) stem with different-sized spacers.

17 Fit the blanks onto the mandrel with the grain lined up correctly, and a spacer gauge in the middle and at either end. Tighten up the locking nut to stop them spinning.

18 Select the top speed on your lathe – somewhere around 3000 rpm is ideal if you can get that high.

19 Although you can buy specialist pen-turning tools, it is quite easy to use standard tools. I find a $^3/4$in (19mm) roughing gouge is actually easier to control than a much smaller one.

20 Bring the blanks down to somewhere near the diameter of the gauge spacers, using the gouge.

21 Then use a skew chisel to reduce it down further, aiming to get as near as possible to the spacer diameter.

22 At your first few attempts you may not be able to get the diameter correct and even straight off the tool, but don't worry unless it is a long way out.

23 You can even things up using some 240 grit abrasive wrapped around a block, but beware of getting the timber too hot or it will crack.

24 Finish off by working down the grades of abrasive; I finish around 800 grit for a really fine surface.

25 There are dedicated pen finishes available but, if you are only making a few, I find that standard cellulose sealer and friction polish leave a very satisfactory surface. Rub in a couple of coats of sealer with the lathe stationary and flat it down with fine abrasive.

26 Apply the friction polish as the lathe is spinning, building up several coats as each one dries.

27 Leave the blanks for several minutes before handling, to allow the polish to harden off properly and avoid finger marks.

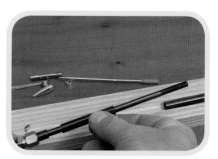

28 Slide the finished barrels off the mandrel, keeping them orientated correctly to each other.

TIP: To keep all the components together and in the right order, make an assembly board with a groove routed along its length to stop them all rolling about.

29 Start the assembly by pressing the pen tip into the bottom end of the first barrel. You can buy dedicated pressers for this, but a standard vice with some soft wooden jaws is fine.

30 Press the mechanism into the top end of the first barrel, making sure it goes in straight.

31 Keep pressing it in until the crimped groove on the mechanism is in line with the end of the barrel.

32 Try screwing in the ink cartridge to see if the nib protrudes enough from the tip. If it doesn't, press the mechanism in a fraction more.

33 Now press the top through the clip into the top end of the second tube.

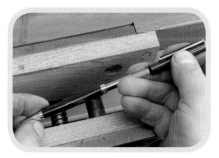

34 Screw in the ink cartridge, then slip on the central ring and push the top on to complete the pen.

The finished pen.

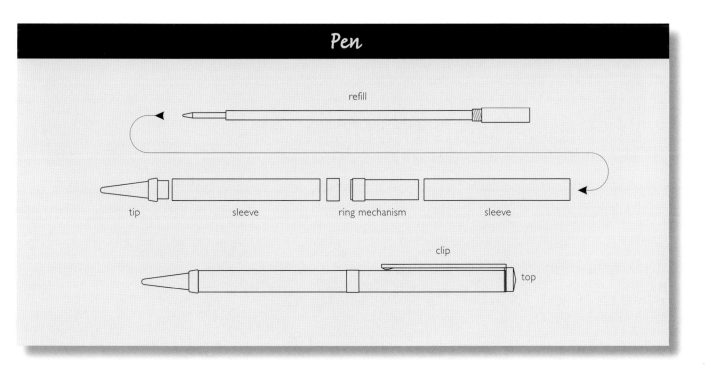

Pen

refill

tip   sleeve   ring mechanism   sleeve

clip   top

Fruit

**Show off the beauty of decorative timbers
by turning fruit that just begs to be handled.**

Everybody loves the tactile quality of wood and a nicely polished sample just has to be handled. I used to make wooden eggs for just this purpose, but even their popularity has now been overtaken by wooden fruits that have all the same appeal but are possibly more decorative.

The fruit can be made from attractive timbers and then polished to highlight the grain, or made from a plain timber and then painted to resemble real fruit. It can also be made from branch wood, particularly those species like yew or laburnum with a stark contrast between the heartwood and sapwood, as the smooth rounded shape accentuates this perfectly.

I cannot see the virtue of mimicking the real thing by painting plain timbers – for me the attraction is using really decorative timber and polishing it to a fine finish.

As natural fruit varies tremendously in shape and size, wooden examples are very easy to turn and you can use offcuts of any size, even tiny bits for grapes and plums. Generally, apples and pears need to be turned from 3 x 3in (76 x 76mm) timber, but use what you have. Miniature or half-scale versions can be just as attractive.

For this project I use just two tools. You can buy special chucks for holding the work, but a simple screwchuck is all you really need and you can easily make this yourself as I shall show you.

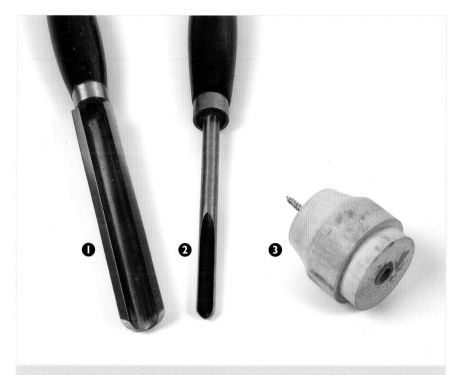

TIP: You could use a standard screwchuck, but these tend to be a bit big and bulky, so it is better to make a lighter dedicated one. All you need is a block of any hardwood about 2 x 2 x 2in (51 x 51 x 51mm) and a suitable No 6 or 8 screw.

TOOLS USED

❶ ³/4in (19mm) roughing gouge   ❷ ³/8in (10mm) spindle gouge
❸ homemade screwchuck

2 Start by turning the blank down to a cylinder, holding it between the centres.

I keep a special box with blanks for making fruit and, whenever I cut down a longer spindle blank, the offcut gets stored in this box for use when I have a fruit-making session.

3 Form a chucking spigot on one end, slightly larger in diameter than the closed diameter of your chuck jaws. This ensures it re-centres accurately every time you use it, and so stops the fruit from wobbling about when you swap it end-to-end later in the turning process.

4 Grip the blank on this spigot and turn the free end to a slight hollow so that the fruit blank will seat down on it properly and not vibrate.

5 Use the drill chuck in the lathe to bore a central hole right through the blank. This hole needs to be slightly smaller in diameter than the diameter of the screw.

6 On the outside of the blank mark the amount the head needs to be countersunk to get the required screw projection – about $^3/4$in (19mm) sticking out. The holes will be disguised in the final stage, so the deeper the better.

7 Counterbore a hole large enough to take the head to the measured depth.

8 Smear the screw with epoxy glue and screw it in firmly until it bottoms in the counterbore.

9 When the glue has set, taper down the projecting end of the screwchuck to allow better access when turning the fruit.

10 Find the centre of your fruit blanks in the conventional way, by drawing in the diagonals.

11 As the screwchuck hold is not very tight, I remove as much of the waste as possible by sawing off the corners on the bandsaw.

12 Drill a suitable pilot hole to take the woodscrew chuck screw. Make sure this is plenty deep enough, you cannot over do it.

13 Screw the blank up tight onto the rim of the screwchuck; you can see now why it is better to make this face slightly concave.

14 Bring up the tailstock for some additional support during the initial shaping stages.

15 A lot of shaping can be carried out with the roughing gouge but use a $^3/_8$in (10mm) spindle gouge for the final profiling.

16 Apples and pears have a dimple in the bottom end, so remove the tailstock and form this shape carefully with the gouge.

17 The top end can only be shaped so far round before you foul on the screwchuck, so just go as far as you can.

18 Use the tailstock chuck again to drill the same-sized pilot hole for the screw in the bottom of the fruit.

19 The fruit must be really well finished and polished to exploit its tactile qualities to the full, so first sand the bottom thoroughly to remove tool marks, working down the grades of abrasive to finish at about 600 grit.

20 Seal the surface with cellulose sanding sealer rubbed in with a cloth whilst the lathe is stationary. After several coats, denib the surface with fine abrasive and then burnish it with 0000 wire wool.

TIP: A coat of friction polish will leave a super-high shine, but this will dull down a little with a lot of handling, so finish off with a light application of carnauba wax on top that can be buffed to a really high gloss.

21 Reverse the finished bottom end onto the wood screw-chuck. Sandwich a piece of cardboard/rubber between the face of the chuck and blank to stop it marking.

22 Now shape the top of the fruit. Again, most fruits have a dimpled top which is easily formed with the spindle gouge, initially using the tailstock for support.

23 Final cuts are made with the tailstock removed.

24 Sand and polish the top area to match the rest of the polished surface. With care, the two can be blended together without a visible 'join' in the finish.

25 Pears are turned in the same way, but you will need a slightly longer blank, something like 4¹/2 x 3 x 3in (114 x 76 x 76mm).

26 This time the shape is more concave than convex. Laburnum branch wood makes particularly striking pears.

27 Stylized lemons can be made in any timber, but for the best yellow effect use satinwood or boxwood.

28 Complete the illusion of real fruit by tidying up the two ends and hiding the screw holes. A clove is a good match for the flower remains at the bottom.

29 Enlarge the drilled hole slightly with a bradawl and then superglue the clove in position.

30 For the stalk, carve your own, salvage real stalks from fruit, or find some fine tree twigs like birch, snip off short lengths and glue them in place.

The finished fruit.

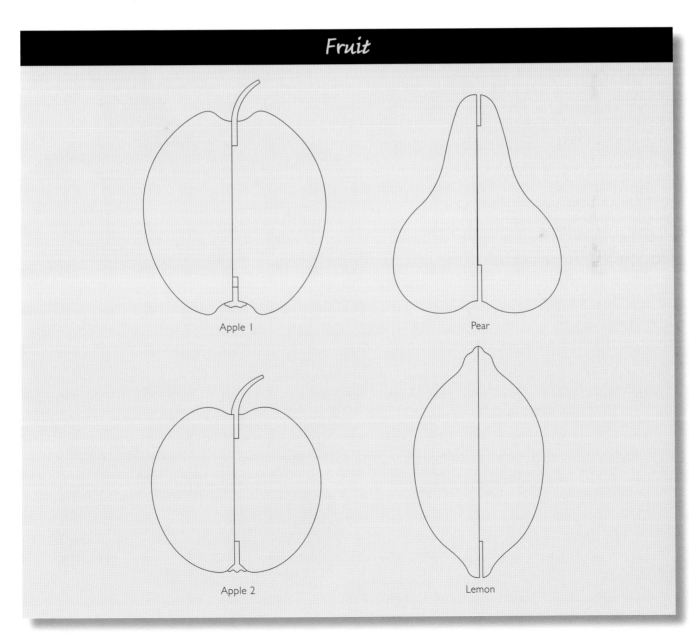

Fruit

Apple 1

Pear

Apple 2

Lemon

Pestle and Mortar

Take the grind out of crushing herbs and spices with a pestle and mortar.

If there are cooks in your house, it won't be long before you are asked to make a pestle and mortar. This ancient utensil is designed to crush up hard seeds and nuts and you have to select the timber carefully, to make sure it is strong enough to withstand the constant pounding.

The timber must be hard and fine grained – maple would be one of the best, but it is virtually impossible to get seriously big pieces that are seasoned well enough. In many cases you will have to restrict yourself to what is available – often log material that you can rough-turn and allow to dry half completed. In this form you can turn the bowl section into the end grain, which is much harder and so more difficult to turn, but is more suited to the purpose.

The alternative is to laminate up a big block from thinner material. However, this is never quite as satisfactory, particularly if you want to turn into the end grain. Laminated blocks always seem to shrink unevenly and the joints end up being highlighted as little steps, not ideal for a food utensil that has to be cleaned.

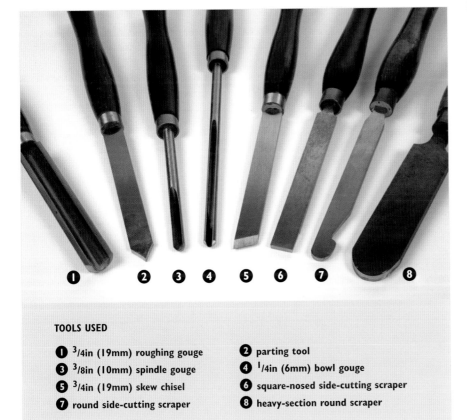

TOOLS USED

① ³/4in (19mm) roughing gouge **②** parting tool
③ ³/8in (10mm) spindle gouge **④** ¹/4in (6mm) bowl gouge
⑤ ³/4in (19mm) skew chisel **⑥** square-nosed side-cutting scraper
⑦ round side-cutting scraper **⑧** heavy-section round scraper

3 Rough down to cylinder, using the ³/4in (19mm) roughing gouge. Approach the spinning timber quite gingerly, until the worst of the remaining corners have gone.

4 True up the ends with a parting tool, making a slightly concave cut and working as close as possible up to the revolving centre.

1 For this project I had the choice of two different blocks. One piece was paler and appeared to be relatively soft with large, open-pored rings. The other was totally different, having tighter, interlocked grain which made it more suitable for this particular use. You will also need a small spindle blank for the pestle which is not shown.

2 The block used for the mortar is approximately 6 x 3³/4 x 3³/4in (152 x 95 x 95mm). Take the corners off the blank on the bandsaw to save time with the roughing out, then mount it securely between centres.

5 To hold such a large block, use the machine woodscrew chuck with maximum projection and large jaws to provide a good bearing surface. Drill the correct size of pilot hole and tighten up securely.

TIP: A tool called 'boa constrictor', which has a rubber strap handle, is ideal for gripping larger-diameter pieces like this, as it gives them that extra amount of tightening that you cannot achieve by hand.

6 Inevitably the blank will not go back on the screwchuck quite true, so use the roughing gouge again to turn it up true again.

7 Use a 1/4in (6mm) bowl gouge to clean up the end grain. (Using a bigger gouge on hard end grain with this amount of overhang from the chuck would probably cause too much chatter.)

8 With a narrow parting tool, form the edge of the chucking recess. This will be hard going in end grain and will probably cause the work to vibrate, so work gently but firmly.

9 Remove the internal waste with the small bowl gouge, making the base of the recess slightly concave to aid accurate rechucking later. Don't bother with fussy detail in the recess, as it all has to be kept clean.

10 To help re-centring, make sure the edge of the recess is dovetailed cleanly, so the jaws seat properly. Use a skew chisel on its side to get the necessary angle.

11 Use the roughing gouge to take away the bulk of the waste in the foot area, then a 3/8in (10mm) spindle gouge to start putting in the detail. There is no tailstock support, so don't take heavy cuts.

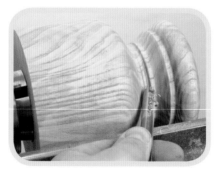

12 For narrow but deep coves where the tool is overhanging the rest a fair way, try using the 1/4in (6mm) bowl gouge for its extra rigidity.

13 To get the straight sides, use the roughing gouge. Pull it backwards from right to left and use your finger as a guide along the toolrest to produce a perfectly straight cut.

14 Keep the external shape very plain and simple, as too much ornamentation in practical kitchen items makes them difficult to clean properly.

15 Sand the whole external profile, working down the grades of abrasive to about 400 grit, slowing the lathe speed down to prevent overheating, which may cause checking in the end grain.

16 Rub in several coats of cellulose sanding sealer with the lathe stationary, flatting down any raised grain between coats with your finest abrasive paper.

17 To produce a super-smooth finish ready for the polish you intend to use, burnish the final surface thoroughly with some 0000 steel wool. For food items, I use several coats of finishing oil, rubbing them in initially with more steel wool and then burnishing with a soft cloth.

18 When the oil has dried, remount the blank on the expanding chuck, twisting it slightly as you tighten up to get it seated accurately.

19 Use a sawtooth bit in the tailstock chuck to drill a central hole to the full hollowing depth. Even a small hole makes the hollowing process so much easier.

20 Start opening out the hole using the small bowl gouge again, working down from the outside edge into the hole with each pass. End-grain work like this is hard work, so resharpen the tool frequently.

21 Once you have done as much as possible with the gouge, switch to a square side-cutting scraper, which cuts on both the end and long edges. Work in small steps to minimize the vibration this causes.

22 Switch to a round-nosed scraper to start blending the square sides into the curved bottom.

TIP: As the tool overhang becomes greater, switch to a large round-nosed scraper to create the smooth internal profile, tipping the tool slightly on its side to shear scrape for a cleaner finish.

23 Use a soft sanding pad in the drill for power sanding the inside, blending the sides and bottom together perfectly, but taking care not to round over the top lip.

24 Finish the inside in the same way as the outside, making sure the oil penetrates well into the end grain. I find the combination of sealer and oil still allows good penetration without getting the blotchy effect associated with using oil on its own.

25 For the pestle I used a piece of mopane, a very hard and durable timber. Grip the blank for the pestle – preferably in a chuck, as it allows free access to one end, but otherwise between centres.

26 Reduce the blank to a cylinder. Very hard timber can be extremely difficult to rough out with a gouge; if you find this, try a round-nosed scraper, as it can leave a much better surface finish.

27 Turn the blank end to end in the chuck, now holding it on the round section for a more secure grip.

28 Turn a smoothly waisted profile with a round section at each end, so the pestle will both grind effectively and be comfortable to hold when pressure is applied.

29 With the main shape complete, remove the tailstock centre and round over the end of the pestle to create a smooth, bulbous contour.

30 Sand as much as possible at this stage, but be careful not to apply too much pressure, or you may lever the blank out of the chuck. Turn down the diameter as small as is practical at the headstock end and then sand and polish the whole thing.

31 | Use a narrow parting tool to cut through and separate the pestle, doing as much of the final shaping as possible as you go.

32 The end of the pestle can then be cleaned up and polished by hand.

The pestle and mortar, ready and waiting for some serious action!

Pestle and Mortar

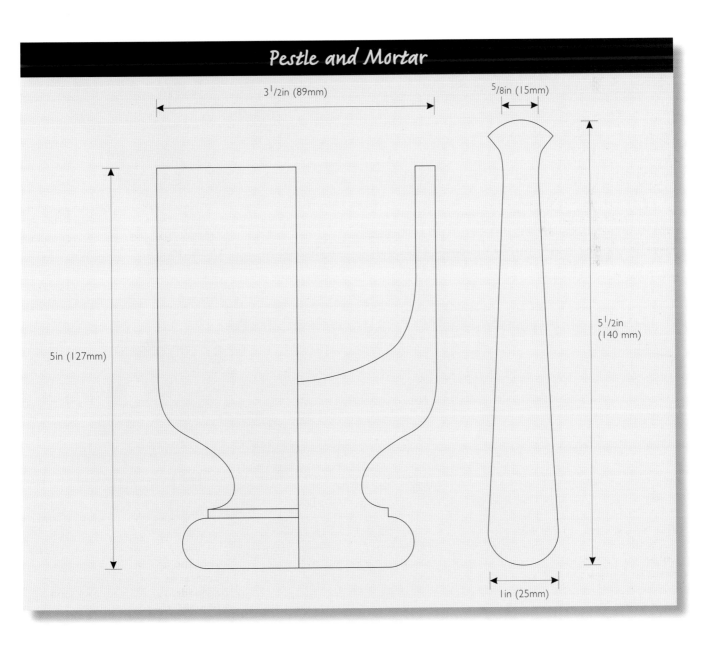

3^1/2in (89mm)

^{5}/8in (15mm)

5in (127mm)

5^1/2in (140 mm)

1in (25mm)

Captive Ring Goblet

Add some interest to an ornamental goblet by adding a couple of captive rings.

Forming captive rings on a project always generates a lot of interest amongst other turners, and to those who are not 'in the know' the conundrum of how the rings have been put in place is even more puzzling.

The procedure is in fact extremely simple: the rings are turned *in situ* from the waste on the spindle and nothing is fitted later. However, the effect is quite decorative and opens up all sorts of possibilities for interesting ornamentation on a whole range of projects, particularly for toys and rattles.

If you intend doing a lot of captive ring work there is actually a range of dedicated beading tools available, but you need a left- and a right-handed one for each size of bead, so it can represent quite an investment if you want to cut a variety of different-sized rings. However, it is possible to cut the rings without having to buy any special tools – a fine parting tool and a skew chisel are all you need, but you will need to take a bit more care to get the rings a consistent size.

To illustrate the technique, I am turning a goblet from a branch of laburnum and leaving two captive rings. Select your timber carefully, finding a branch that is split-free and as straight as possible. Fine-textured timbers like laburnum or yew are ideal, as they will take the fine detail better and are stronger in the tiny cross-grain areas of the finished rings.

TOOLS USED

❶ ³/4in (19mm) roughing gouge ❷ standard parting tool
❸ ³/8in (10mm) spindle gouge ❹ ¹/4in (6mm) spindle gouge
❺ ³/4in (19mm) skew chisel ❻ round-nosed side-cutting scraper
❼ square-nosed side-cutting scraper ❽ miniature parting tool

1 Timbers which have distinctly coloured heartwood and sapwood provide a really striking contrast when turned from the log section.

2 Start by finding the centre of the branch, using a compass to draw the maximum diameter circle. Take a good guess if the section is very irregular.

3 Mount the blank between centres and spin it by hand a few times, to check that all is clear and reasonably well balanced before you start the lathe.

4 Also before you start, peel away any large patches of loose or flaking bark to minimize the amount of flying debris, and anyway always wear eye protection.

5 With the lathe spinning at about 1000 rpm rough down to a cylinder using a ³/4in (19mm) gouge. If the blank has not been centred too well, reposition one end to try and balance it up.

6 Mark out at one end for a gripping spigot; for maximum grip, make it just a fraction bigger than the true diameter of the chuck jaws, and undercut the shoulder a little to provide a firm seating.

TIP: Use extended 'shark' jaws fitted to your chuck to provide enough support for the long blank and stop it levering out. The spigot must be as long as possible, with the shoulder being a snug fit against the end of the jaws. The end of the blank must not 'bottom' on the chuck body.

7 With the blank now secured in the chuck, bring up the tailstock for support, trim up the end and re-true the cylinder if it isn't quite centred.

8 Form the basic shape of the cup section using a $^3/_8$in (10mm) spindle gouge, well over on its side, to make clean slicing cuts.

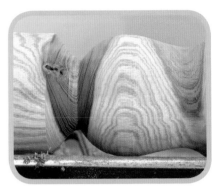

9 Don't undercut the cup too much at this stage or you will weaken it, resulting in a lot more vibration during the hollowing stage.

10 Use a drill in the tailstock to bore down to the required hollowing depth. A sawtooth bit cuts a clean hole and quickly removes a lot of the waste.

11 The initial hollowing can be carried out with a $^1/_4$in (6mm) spindle gouge but, whilst this cuts cleanly, it will start to vibrate as the overhang becomes greater.

12 The deeper hollowing is best carried out with a thick, square-ended scraper; I use one that cuts on both the side and the end.

13 Take light cuts to minimize the vibration, gradually nibbling away at the waste and stopping occasionally to remove the swarf that gets trapped in the bowl.

14 To blend the sides into the base, use a round-nosed scraper sharpened well up the side and aim for a nicely U-shaped profile in the base of the goblet.

15 Once the hollowing is complete, finish off the outer profile and make any necessary refinements to get the wall thickness even.

16 Form the detail at the base of the cup and then reduce the stem area to match the outer diameter of the finished ring. I put in a fixed bead to mimic the rings.

17 Make a parting cut either side of the first ring, leaving yourself plenty of room to manoeuvre.

18 Form the top shape of the ring using a small skew or a parting tool, rolling it either way to produce a bead.

19 The ideal tool for releasing the ring is a very narrow parting tool, though some turners do it all with a skew.

20 Undercut the bead from one side first, trying to maintain the rounded shape.

21 Then repeat from the other side, gradually taking a bit more from each side.

22 If the parting tool is hollow ground, you can use it flat, as a scraper, to reach round the back of the ring from either side.

23 Eventually only a tiny centre skin is left to support the ring, so make a final cut with the parting tool to slice through this.

24 Stop the lathe and check that the ring is properly free and has no damage; you can break it off and turn another if there is any serious chipping.

25 I wanted two rings, so just repeated the whole procedure to form the second one. Aim to match their size and shape as closely as possible.

TIP: To clean up the inside of the rings, turn the remaining spindle dead flat and stick some fine abrasive paper onto it to act as a temporary drum sander.

26 Hold the rings and set the lathe to run slowly, so you can sand the inside edge to a smooth profile.

27 When the rings are cleaned up properly, peel away the abrasive, ready to shape the rest of the spindle and base.

28 Before you weaken it all any more, sand the bowl section, working down the grades to about 400 grit.

29 To keep the rings out of the way whilst you do the rest of the shaping, wedge them in place with some folded abrasive paper, or an elastic band.

30 Shape up the base and stem, but be prepared for the bowl to start wobbling off centre a little, as the wood warps when the drying stresses are released.

31 Sand the whole goblet carefully, working around the rings and ensuring that they don't snag in the abrasive paper. Apply several coats of sanding sealer.

32 Burnish the last coat of sealer with 0000 wire wool, then apply a pastewax and buff with a soft cloth. The rings will have to be hand polished.

33 Carefully part the goblet off from the remaining waste in the chuck. If you are not confident about parting right through whilst it's spinning, use a saw with the lathe stationary for the last bit.

34 Shape the remaining bit of waste to be a tight fit in the mouth of the goblet. This will act as a friction chuck for the base to be finished off.

35 With the goblet back between centres, shape the underside of the base, then polish it, finishing off the final centre pip by hand.

The completed goblet with both rings still intact – quite a transformation from a scruffy piece of branch wood.

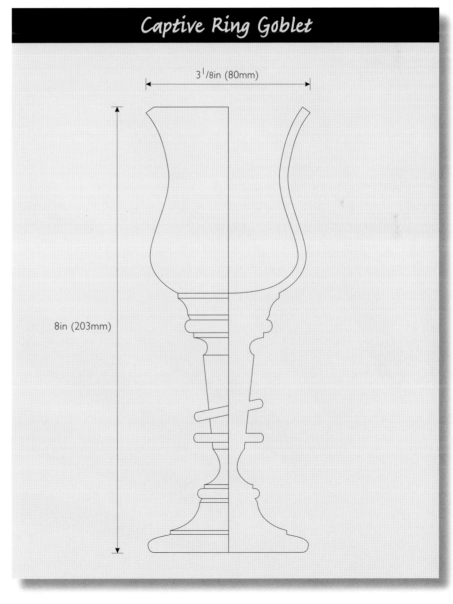

Captive Ring Goblet

3 1/8in (80mm)

8in (203mm)

Garden Accessories

Bring some style to the potting shed with beautiful hand-turned garden accessories.

If you have friends or relatives who are keen gardeners, one or more of these simple projects will always be well received. They make fantastic presents and their finished look belies the relatively small amount of time and work needed to make them. No precise measurements are involved and you can turn them to whatever size you fancy, depending on the available timber.

There is a selection of dibbers, a pot presser and a string line holder. All of them are very quick to make and are an ideal way of using up some of those pieces of small branch wood that seem to accumulate under the workbench. Often these branches are too small in diameter for much else, but are ideal material for these projects.

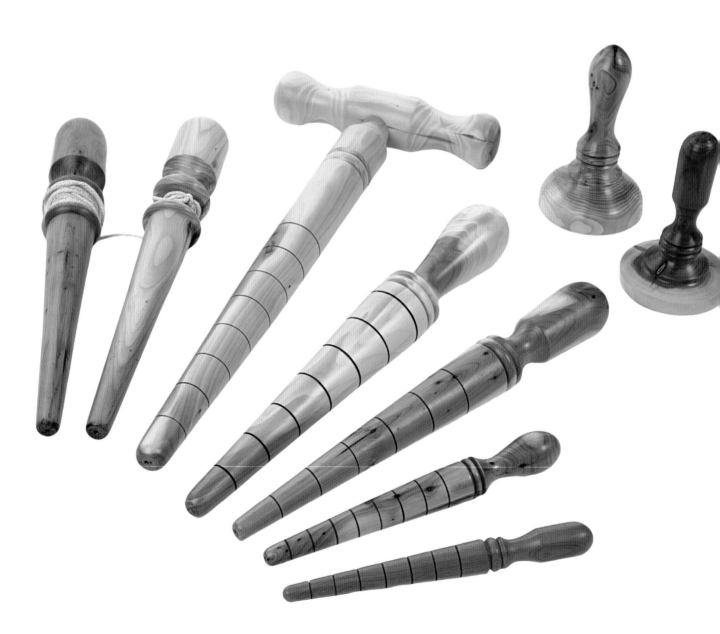

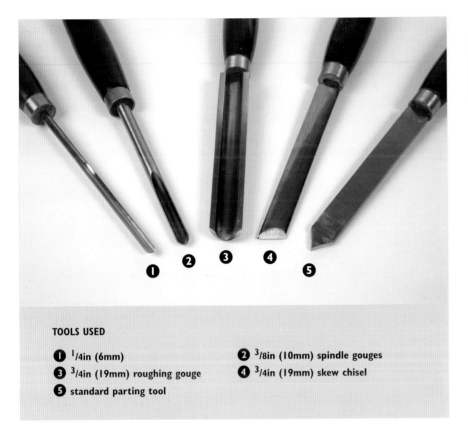

TOOLS USED

❶ ¹/4in (6mm)

❷ ³/8in (10mm) spindle gouges

❸ ³/4in (19mm) roughing gouge

❹ ³/4in (19mm) skew chisel

❺ standard parting tool

STRAIGHT DIBBER
For this I used up some yew
branches that I'd nearly thrown
away, thinking they were useless.
However, yew is a beautiful raw
material and this project shows
that it is worth keeping any odd bits.

2 Choose a suitable piece of
straight branch wood and
make sure the ends are cut
reasonably square. With irregular
shapes like this you have to guess
where the centre point is, but it is
usually not that critical.

3 Mount the work between centres.
Before you start the lathe, turn it
by hand, to make sure there are
no protruding knots or branches likely
to foul on the toolrest. As the branch
is so irregular in shape, with varying
amounts of heartwood and sapwood,
it is unlikely to be very well balanced,
so first set the lathe at a lower speed
than normal, to see how smoothly it
rotates. If all is well, try increasing the
speed up to about 2000 rpm for small
sections like this.

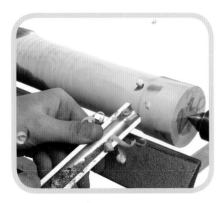

4 Using a ³/4in (19mm) roughing-out gouge, approach the work carefully from the right end. Move the gouge a bit more to the left with each cut and, as you near the left end of the timber, reposition the toolrest and start working off that end.

TIP: As branch sections are so irregular and bent, you will often find that you are taking a lot more from one side than the other. If the discrepancy is marked, try readjusting the tailstock centre position to balance it up a bit.

5 Keep working away like this until you have reduced the branch to a perfect cylinder. Remember to move the rest in close to the work as the roughing out proceeds, or you'll soon end up with a lot of tool overhang.

6 The roughing gouge can be used for a lot of the basic shaping and, now that the blank is better balanced, you should be able to increase the speed to about 2500 rpm. To get to a nice parallel taper for the main part of the dibber, it helps to twist the toolrest to the necessary angle and then use it as a guide to form the correct taper.

7 The long tapered section can be smoothed off using a skew chisel; practise swinging the handle up and down to vary the width of cut and quality of finish.

8 The top end of the dibber can be rounded over using the spindle gouge to leave just a small nib at the drive-centre end. This can then be cleaned off by hand as the last operation.

9 The shaping of the handle is a matter of personal preference. It doesn't need to be too ornate but a few small details are necessary to make it look attractive. I settled on a style that could be re-produced on all the other items to make them look like a set.

10 Once you are happy with the shape, check the taper for straightness using a small steel rule or straightedge, and make any necessary adjustments with the skew chisel.

TIP: To clean up these straight sections, wrap some fine abrasive taper around a block of wood and run this up and down the length as the work revolves. It is often better to reduce the lathe speed for sanding fine-grained timbers like yew, as they can soon overheat and develop small heat checks.

11 To give some indication of planting depths, mark out 1in (25mm) graduations along the taper.

12 Next, cut a small groove at each pencil line, using a skew chisel to delineate them clearly.

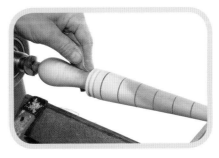

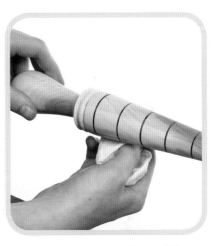

13 To enhance the lines, blacken them with a wire burner. Apply a lot of pressure, so it is hot enough to scorch the wood. Never wrap the wire round your fingers; ideally fit wooden handles at each end.

14 Sand well all over, but for projects like this that are soon going to get dirty, there is no point spending hours getting a perfect finish. Working down to about 320 grit is more than enough.

15 Leave the wood unpolished if you like, but I prefer to work in a couple of coats of cellulose sealer, flatting down well between each coat, and then to finish off with a coat of melamine lacquer. This gives a water-resistant and generally impervious finish that looks attractive, but will inevitably get a little dirty with use.

16 Use the skew chisel to part through the tiny nib at the headstock end and just blend this in by hand with abrasive.

17 SMALL DIBBER
The small dibber is ideal for work with seedlings and the procedure for making it is exactly the same as for the larger one. However, it is often more difficult to hold these small sections adequately, so I just grip them between a ring centre in the headstock and a standard revolving centre.

18 The turning sequence is much the same as for the bigger version, still using the 3/4in (19mm) roughing gouge.

19 Again use the skew chisel to form the straight taper, then make the depth graduations, but for smaller dibbers space these at 1/2in (13mm) intervals.

20 POT PRESSER
This is an equally simple project. It could be turned from two separate pieces, but I find it much quicker and more economical to make it from one single piece, rather than worry about the waste.

21 To start with, hold the blank between centres, and rough down to a cylinder. As the large end has to be turned perfectly flat, you need to grip the blank so that this end is accessible and not supported by the tailstock.

22 To achieve this, turn a small spigot on one end of the blank that can be gripped in your combination chuck. Make sure the spigot shoulder is parallel and slightly undercut at the shoulder for a firm grip.

23 Bring the tailstock back up to give support for as long as possible, then start turning away the bulk of the waste to form the handle of the presser.

24 With the bulk of the waste removed, start adding the detail; don't overdo it, but a little simple decoration makes the finished project more appealing. Notice how the handle profile is similar to that on the dibbers.

25 Before you reduce the diameter of the handle too much, remove the tailstock and clean up the end of the presser, to get it perfectly flat, using a small spindle gouge or the skew chisel.

26 Sand and polish in exactly the same way as before, but do be careful, as there is only a small amount of support at the end of the handle and this is easily snapped if you press too hard.

27 With the polishing completed, part off by slicing through with the skew. Alternatively, if you are not too confident about parting a revolving workpiece, use a fine saw with the lathe stationary.

28 STRING LINE HOLDERS These are very much like the large dibber, the only complication being that you have to produce two the same. The first one is easy to turn, so use this as a template for the second one. Provided the main dimensions are all the same the rest of the detail will look surprisingly similar, just keep holding them up against each other to check progress as the turning proceeds. Once again the handle shape is reproduced at the top end, with a smaller-diameter section bounded by two beads to form a reservoir for the string.

29 TEE-HANDLED DIBBER This dibber is very similar to the standard version, but it is on a larger scale and has the additional handle for easier planting of crops like leeks, which require a much deeper hole.

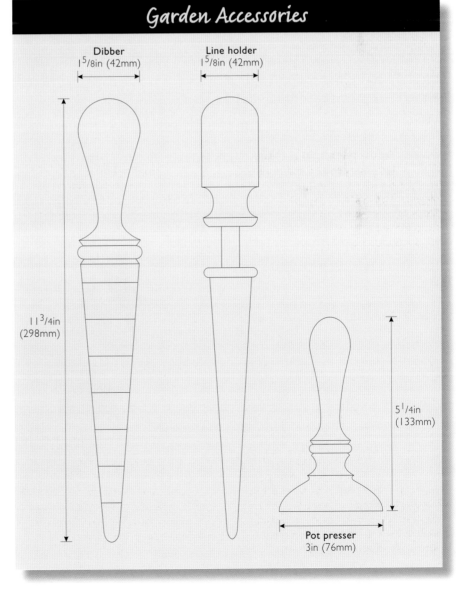

Garden Accessories

Dibber
$1^5/8$in (42mm)

Line holder
$1^5/8$in (42mm)

$11^3/4$in (298mm)

$5^1/4$in (133mm)

Pot presser
3in (76mm)

Earring Stand

Make one of these elegant stands to tame all those wayward earrings that seem to accumulate all over the house.

Earring stands are another good item for selling at craft fairs and this two-tiered version has proved to be even more popular than a single-tiered one. The stand does not have to be made this big – in fact a very small one, to take just a few pairs of earrings, is an excellent way to use up some smaller offcuts.

The design is not critical either, but don't make it too heavy-looking and make sure that the holes for the earring stems are not too far in from the edge, or you will struggle to thread on some of the pendant-style earrings.

Timber choice is again not too important, but finer-grained species that can take the small detail are always better. In this example I have used a block of beefwood and turned the whole stand from the single block. Making it up from several pieces would be less wasteful, but this would take longer and it is tricky to get the colour and grain of the separate pieces to match, unless you cut them all from the same blank.

Using a single block will require some prior thought as to how it will be held securely at the various stages. There are lots of other ways, but the method described here works for me.

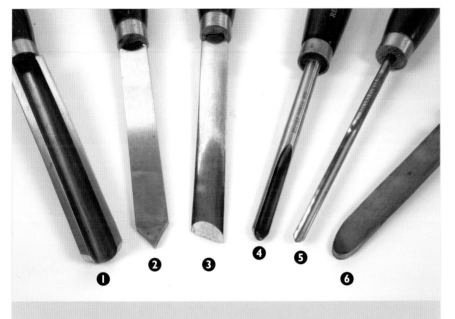

TOOLS USED

1 roughing gouge
3 3/4in (19mm) skew chisel
5 1/4in (6mm) spindle gouge

2 parting tool
4 3/8in (10mm) spindle gouge
6 round-nosed scraper

3 Remove the corners using the 3/4in (19mm) roughing gouge, working from the right-hand end and coming back a bit further to the left for each successive cut.

4 With the corners removed, a large gap opens up between the blank and the rest, so move it closer for maximum tool support and increase the speed to about 2000 rpm.

1 For a two-tiered stand, start with a block 7 x 3 1/2 x 3 1/2in (178 x 89 x 89mm) and mount it securely between centres, setting the lathe speed to about 1500 rpm.

2 Bring the toolrest as close as possible, checking that it is securely locked and that the wood spins freely.

5 Now mount the blank in the chuck: use the parting tool to turn a gripping spigot at the tailstock end, making this spigot diameter just a fraction bigger than the close diameter of the jaws.

6 Trim the spigot until it is perfectly parallel. Undercut the shoulder slightly to maximize the grip, as there will be a fair bit of leverage on the blank when you start working on the end.

7 Provided the spigot isn't too long, the shoulder on the blank will sit up tight against the chuck jaws and stop it wobbling about. Getting the work really secure is half the battle with woodturning.

8 Use a parting tool to trim up the end of the blank and get it balanced, taking light cuts to minimize any deep tearing on the end grain.

9 Mark out for the chucking recess, again only taking light cuts, as the tool and wood will vibrate excessively if you press too hard.

10 Clean out the waste with a small spindle gouge, making the base of the recess at least perfectly flat, but preferably slightly concave, so that the chuck fits in square.

11 With all these chucking recesses it is important to get the inside edge slightly dovetailed to match the jaw profile, so cut it back at a slight angle, using the skew chisel flat on its side as a small scraper.

12 Sand and polish the inside of this recess, then the flat part of the base, as you will not be able to access it again after this stage.

13 Now turn the work round and expand the chuck jaws out to grip in the finished recess.

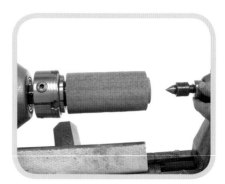

TIP: Bring the tailstock back up to provide some extra support for as long as possible. This is not strictly necessary, but it does allow you to make heavier cuts and therefore speeds up the turning process.

14 Use the parting tool to mark out the position of all the main detail, cutting well in to somewhere near the required final diameters.

15 Quickly cut away the obvious waste with the roughing gouge, but take care around the two thin earring carriers – leave them slightly over thickness, as they have a lot of weak short grain and are easily snapped off.

16 Complete the more detailed roughing out using a $^3/_8$in (10mm) spindle gouge.

17 Again, leave plenty of support for the carriers at this stage, but cut away enough to allow them to be drilled through easily.

18 Use the point of the skew to scribe a reference line in about $^3/_{16}$in (5mm) from the outer edge of each carrier.

TIP: If you have a dividing head on your lathe, it is easy to set out the drilling positions. If you don't have this luxury, use a pair of dividers to step around the previously scribed line, adjusting the setting of the dividers until you start and end up in the same place. Check that you have an even number of holes and readjust the spacing if not.

19 When you are happy with the spacing, use a bradawl to clearly mark the position of each hole and to ensure the drill centres accurately, as they must be spot on to look right.

20 The easiest way to drill the holes accurately is on a drill press, but you can do it by hand with a power drill if you are careful. The hole only needs to be $^5/_{64}$in (2mm) in diameter.

21 With the holes all drilled, use the gouge to take a fine cut off the top and bottom faces of the carriers, to clean up any ragging and to make them look a bit more delicate – but don't make them too thin, or they will break away around the holes.

22 The fine detail of the stem can now be worked with the $^1/_4$in (6mm) spindle gouge and the parting tool. Keep up the support from the tailstock for the moment. If the carriers make it difficult to access the spindle with a gouge, use a small round-nosed scraper instead.

23 Hollow out the saucer shape in the base with the spindle gouge. This is the ideal place for storing spare earring backs.

24 Reduce the lathe speed to about 1200 rpm and sand the profile carefully. Work progressively down the grades and finish off at about 400 grit.

25 At the last moment, complete the shaping at the tailstock end, moving it completely out of the way for the final cuts.

26 Now sand this area to match the rest but, because of the relatively small amount of support from the chuck on a long piece like this, don't press too hard.

27 The completed profile ready for finishing. I prefer a high gloss on small, delicate pieces like this and use friction polish or wax. If you prefer a less glossy finish, use an oil finish.

28 Whatever the finish, the first stage should be several coats of cellulose sanding sealer rubbed in with the lathe stationary and flatted down between coats with fine abrasive.

29 After you have completed all the sanding and sealing, but before you apply the final polish, clean out the holes by carefully running the drill bit through them again.

30 The final finish on this stand is a coat of pastewax, rubbed in with a soft cloth, then buffed with the lathe spinning at about 2000 rpm.

The finished stand.

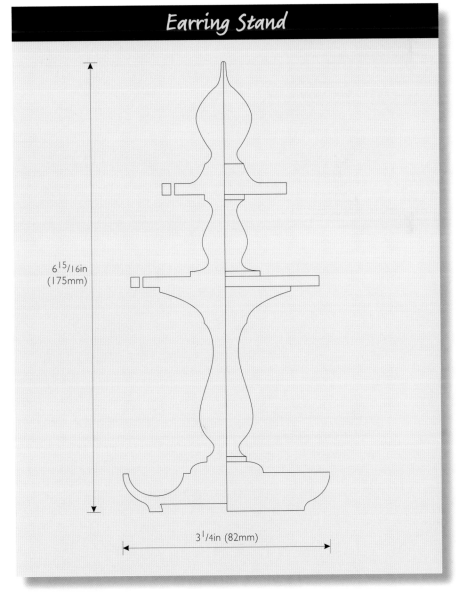

Earring Stand

$6^{15}/16$in (175mm)

$3^{1}/4$in (82mm)

Scoop

Bring a touch of natural elegance to the kitchen with a beautiful wooden scoop.

Scoops are another great way of using up all those odds and ends of timber that are too good to throw away. Even better is the fact that they are extremely quick and easy to turn, and who could refuse the gift of a beautifully hand-turned scoop, whether a tiny one for condiments or larger one for general use?

Whatever size, a scoop is always a useful and decorative item to have around the kitchen. For this medium-sized one, I am starting with an olive blank 2^1/$_2$ x 2^1/$_2$ x 8in (64 x 64 x 203mm), but you can make them from any species, provided it hollows easily on the end grain.

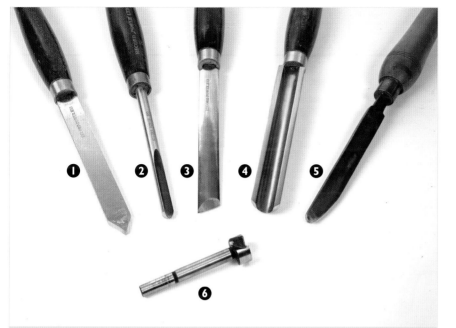

TOOLS USED

❶ parting tool
❸ 3/4in (19mm) skew chisel
❺ round-nosed scraper

❷ 3/8in (10mm) spindle gouge
❹ 3/4in (19mm) roughing gouge
❻ 1in (25mm) sawtooth bit

3 However, do check the clearance from the toolrest. To do this, spin it a few times by hand before you start, just in case it is not square.

4 Rough out with a shallow-section 3/4in (19mm) gouge, with the lathe at about 2000 rpm, but take it slowly and wear suitable eye protection during the roughing-out process.

1 The block is initially between centres in the conventional way, so draw in the diagonals to get the centre point.

2 Knock in the drive centre using a wooden mallet, 1/8in (2 or 3mm) penetration should be sufficient for a small block like this.

5 Start roughing from the right-hand end. Work down to the middle and then swap the gouge round to finish off working the left-hand end.

6 To grip the scoop for turning, either use a combination chuck with gripping jaws of about the same diameter as the roughed-out blank, or turn one end of the cylinder down to a spigot that matches the diameter of the jaws.

7 Use callipers to get this diameter right, as the closer the spigot is to the jaw diameter the better the grip will be.

8 Take special care with the shoulder of the spigot and undercut it slightly, so the jaws will sit up tight and prevent the blank wobbling about.

TIP: When you are fitting big, heavy chucks on the lathe, make sure they are properly tightened up on the spindle before you start the lathe. If they are even a fraction loose, the initial inertia will cause them to screw on so tight that they become almost impossible to remove.

9 Tighten up on the spigot, making sure the wood is in square and the shoulder is touching all around the jaws.

10 I prefer to start forming the outer profile of the scoop using the $^3/_8$in (10mm) gouge. Other turners do the hollowing first and then shape the outer profile to match, but I find this makes it more difficult to check the finished shape.

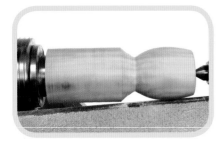

11 However, don't weaken the neck section below the cup too much at this stage or it will vibrate excessively as you try and do the hollowing.

TIP: The next stage is to hollow out for the cup of the scoop, and you can get a good start with this by using a sawtooth bit in the tailstock. You will need to reduce the speed a bit for sawtooth boring, depending on the diameter of the bit. I go down to about 750 rpm for a 1in (25mm) diameter bit. It is so much easier to hollow out end grain like this if there is an initial hole to work into.

12 Very few tailstock barrels are graduated for drilling. If yours isn't and you want to measure how deep you have drilled, start the drilling process with the barrel drawn back flush to the end of the casting.

13 To get an accurate indication of depth, simply measure how much barrel is becoming exposed as you drill.

14 The initial hollowing is carried out with a ³/8in (10mm) spindle gouge used well on its side to keep the tool bevel rubbing.

15 Eventually you won't be able to reach in far enough with the gouge, so swap to a round-nosed scraper. I prefer a specially shaped one that has its cutting edge right up the side as well as the end. Pushing it straight into the wood often causes a lot of chatter and vibration, so instead use it by pulling outwards from the centre, to give a much smoother and more even cut.

16 The critical feature of a scoop is to get the walls thin and as parallel as possible. This means that when you cut the side away to form the scoop shape, the remaining edge is even in thickness down its length. A very slight taper is acceptable, but if you cut into one with very thickly tapered walls the result is a very clumsy-looking affair, so use callipers to keep checking on the wall thickness as you work.

17 Finish off by blending the sides into the bottom with the scraper. Don't press too hard at any stage of the hollowing process, as there is a lot of leverage on the chuck jaws, so go gently or you will pull the work out of the chuck. Steady the side with your left hand as you work to minimize the vibration. Tilting the scraper on its side to produce a shear cut also helps improve the finish.

18 The biggest problem with any deep hollowing is the accumulation of shavings inside the cup, which tend to obscure your view. The only real answer is to keep stopping the lathe to clear them out, particularly when you start getting near to the finished size.

19 Now shape the outside to the final profile, put in the neck detail with a skew if you want to access underneath the base of the cup section.

20 When you are happy with the cup section, sand it thoroughly whilst there is still plenty of support from the rest of the timber. Beware of overheating by pressing too hard with the abrasive, as this can cause little heat checks to form in the end grain which may split the bowl. Work down the grades of abrasive from about 180 grit to 400 to give a really fine finish. Wipe over the inside with a food-safe oil finish.

21 With the cup section complete, start to form the handle, using the roughing gouge again to remove the bulk of the waste. The bowl section may start to go off centre a little as you reduce the stem. This is quite normal and is the result of any drying stresses in the wood being released as you turn – another good reason to finish the bowl end before you complete the stem.

22 Swap to the spindle gouge when you need to refine the shape, turning away as much of the waste at the chuck end as possible.

23 Grip a small piece of waste in the chuck and turn a spigot on this to be a jam fit in the bowl of the scoop. This needs to be tight, but not so tight that you split the bowl, so keep stopping the lathe and trying it for a push fit.

24 Once the scoop is securely pressed on, you can complete the shaping of the handle properly.

25 Use a skew chisel or spindle gouge to round over the end, but for now leave a small stub on the end for support from the tailstock centre.

26 Now sand as much as possible of the outside profile, working down the grades and finishing off with 400 grit abrasive.

27 As a finish, I always use a straightforward food-safe oil, as it is not over glossy but is very safe and practical, but you could use melamine for a glossier and more durable surface.

28 To part off the scoop, either cut through the remaining stub using a handsaw or, if you are more confident, use the parting tool or skew chisel.

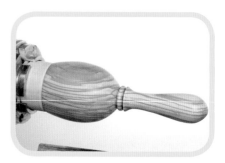

29 Carefully give this cut surface a light sand and polish as it spins, supported just on the jam chuck.

30 You now need to cut away a large portion of the bowl to produce the scoop shape. If you hold it carefully from behind the blade, this is easily accomplished on the bandsaw. The actual shape is a matter of personal taste, but I like to cut plenty away.

31 Once it is cut, you can now see why it is so necessary to get the wall thickness even, as any irregularity will show up immediately.

32 Round over the cut edge into a smooth flowing curve, ideally on a belt sander.

33 Blend in the sharp edges of the bowl by hand with some fine abrasive paper.

The finished scoop. What a pleasure it will be to use.

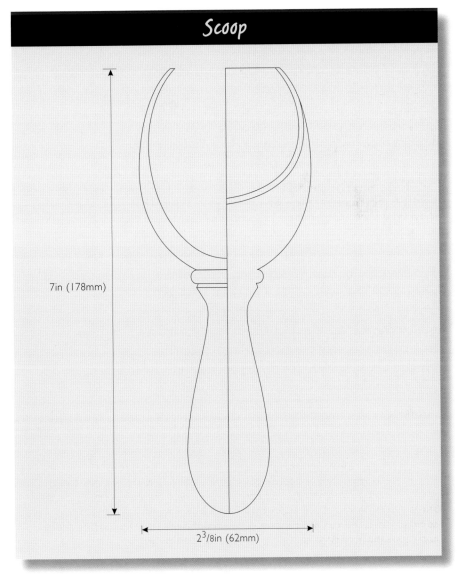

Scoop

7in (178mm)

$2^{3}/8$in (62mm)

Peppermill

**Spice up your cooking with a bespoke peppermill in the timber of your choice.
This design is very traditional, but you can vary it to suit.**

A peppermill is an attractive as well as a functional piece of woodturning. The finished result looks quite complicated, but the actual turning is very simple, although it does require accurate working at all stages if the mill is to function properly when you put it together. The main problem is that it consists of two shaped pieces, both of which have to be held so that they can be turned at either end. I have found the method described to be the easiest, if you have a combination chuck with the relevant jaws. Try it this way first, but then alter the method to suit your own ideas and equipment.

The mechanism is a fairly standard 7in (178mm) one, which most woodworking suppliers stock in a variety of different lengths. I would suggest you don't choose anything too long to start with, to keep the drilling process simpler at this stage. Take some time to study the various components to understand how it all fits together and works. If it is your first attempt, it is not a bad idea to draw it out full size before you start, to make sure you know what goes where, as there is very little room for alteration if you get any of the sizes wrong during the turning. The exact dimensions will vary depending on the type of mill you use, but the principle is exactly the same with them all.

I used ash for this mill, as it turns well and the strong grain always looks good on small, rounded profiles like this. You can use virtually any timber, but avoid those like oak, chestnut and olive which react badly to contact with the metal parts of the mill. You don't need to allow for much waste: about $1/2$in (13mm) on the finished length should be plenty.

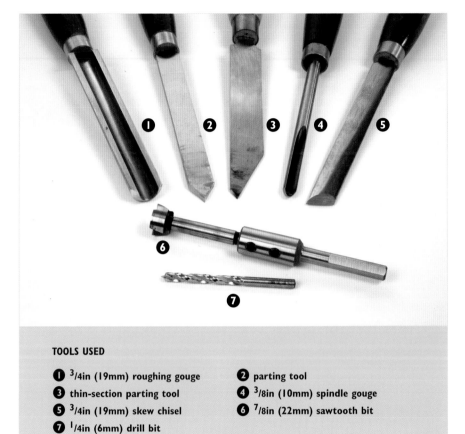

TOOLS USED

❶ ³/4in (19mm) roughing gouge
❷ parting tool
❸ thin-section parting tool
❹ ³/8in (10mm) spindle gouge
❺ ³/4in (19mm) skew chisel
❻ ⁷/8in (22mm) sawtooth bit
❼ ¹/4in (6mm) drill bit

2 For this mill, the blank I used was $7^1/2 \times 2^1/2 \times 2^1/2$in (190 x 63 x 63mm). Mark the centre of the blank, either by drawing in the diagonals, or by using a centre finder.

Set out all the components of the mill, as these have to be fitted precisely and you don't want to miss anything out.

3 Knock in the drive centre. Use a wooden mallet or a soft-faced hammer, as a metal hammer would burr the end of the centre and prevent it seating accurately in the Morse taper of the spindle.

4 Mount the blank between centres, bring the toolrest up as close as possible without it fouling on the spinning blank, and revolve it a couple of times by hand to check this clearance.

5 Remove the corners with the roughing gouge. It is important to keep the handle well down to get the bevel contact and so ensure smooth cutting. Lathe speed should be about 1500 rpm if the blank is well balanced.

6 Reduce the length to a nicely parallel cylinder; don't worry if there are a few small flats left on it at this stage, as there is still a lot more shaping to do.

7 The top will need to be gripped in a chuck when it is parted off, so turn a gripping spigot on this end, sizing it carefully to match your chuck jaws.

8 Undercut the shoulder of this spigot slightly to improve its location and grip in the chuck.

9 To minimize any grain discontinuity in the finished mill, use a thin-gauge parting tool to separate the top and bottom sections, widening the groove slightly as you cut in to prevent the tool binding and overheating.

10 Part through to within $^{1}/_{2}$in (12mm) or so and then stop the lathe and finish off the cut using a fine handsaw. This is much safer than parting right through when both ends are supported between the centres.

11 Re-grip the lower portion of the blank in the chuck, with what will be the bottom end facing outwards.

12 Now bore a $^{7}/_{8}$in (22mm) hole using a sawtooth bit held in the tailstock chuck. Correct lathe speed is very important here because we are deep drilling down the grain and if you spin the work too fast the bit will burn, so ideally reduce the speed to about 700 rpm. The bit must be really sharp for end-grain work, so keep withdrawing it to clear the build-up of swarf behind, otherwise it will clog and be very difficult to remove.

TIP: Bore about halfway in from this end, but you will find that the amount of traverse on most tailstocks is not sufficient to bore deep enough in one go, so stop the lathe and reposition the tailstock further, after you have drilled so far. When you have finished, take the drill out of the tailstock – don't just slide it back out of the way, or you will catch you elbow on it during the next stage.

13 Put the speed back up to about 2000 rpm and use the skew chisel on its side to carefully open out the bore to take the plastic peppercorn holder, which is normally about 1in (25mm) in diameter. Next, form the rebates for the bottom parts of the grinder and its retaining plate.

14 Clean up the remaining end section using a gouge, slightly tapering the cut inwards so that the mill will sit firm.

15 Make a trial fit of all the components, in particular making sure they fit in deep enough so that the retaining screws won't stick out when it's all assembled.

16 Sand and polish this end and then reverse the blank onto the long-nosed chuck jaws. Expand them out to give a really secure grip.

17 Now you can complete the drilling from this end with the 7/8in (22mm) bit, withdrawing it frequently to clear the swarf. As you pull it back, keep your hand on the drill chuck to ensure that it is not pulled out of the Morse taper.

18 For additional support turn a slightly tapered wooden plug to fit into the hole you have just drilled, so that you can bring up the tailstock for the rest of the shaping.

19 Pull the blank off the chuck slightly, so you can turn right up to the end without the tools fouling on the chuck.

20 Use the roughing gouge to cut away the bulk of the waste. You can actually do most of the shaping with this tool, as it is easier to control on long, flat areas.

21 The beads at the bottom can be formed with the parting tool, used as a small skew chisel, but beware of catching the top, unsupported edge, or the tool will dig in.

22 Make a slicing cut across the top end with the skew, again tapering it in slightly so the top will fit up snug.

23 Now grip the top section in the chuck, gripping down on the spigot you formed earlier, and turn down another spigot to be a tight fit in the $^7/8$in (22mm) bore.

24 This top should be a tight friction fit in the bore. You should have to tap it in with your hand, but don't make it so tight that you split the bottom.

25 Once again, bring up the tailstock for some additional support whilst you shape the top using the $^3/8$in (10mm) spindle gouge, rolling it over to form a big bead.

26 Remove the tailstock for the final finishing cuts, slicing across the end grain with the skew chisel on its back.

27 Drill a $^1/4$in (6mm) hole right through the top to take the long stem of the mill. This should be a clearance fit, but it doesn't need to be tight.

28 Sand the whole outer profile. Work progressively down the grades of abrasive to finish at about 400 grit, maybe even finer for some of the exotic timbers.

29 Rub in several of coats of cellulose sanding sealer and flat down the surface with 400 grit abrasive after each coat has dried. Coarse-grained timbers like this ash will probably need three coats.

TIP: If your lathe is fitted with reverse, try flatting in alternate directions, burnishing the final coat with 0000 steel wool to leave a super-smooth surface for polishing.

30 I prefer melamine as a finish, as it has good wear resistance and is also water resistant. You can either spray it or apply it with a cloth, building up two or three coats for a more durable surface.

31 When the polish is dry, remove the top and lightly hand sand the inside of the top of the main bore. This slackens off the fit of the top, so that it turns freely in the body to make the grinder operate.

32 Assemble all the parts, fixing the top capstan plate and the bottom grinding mechanism with the small screws provided.

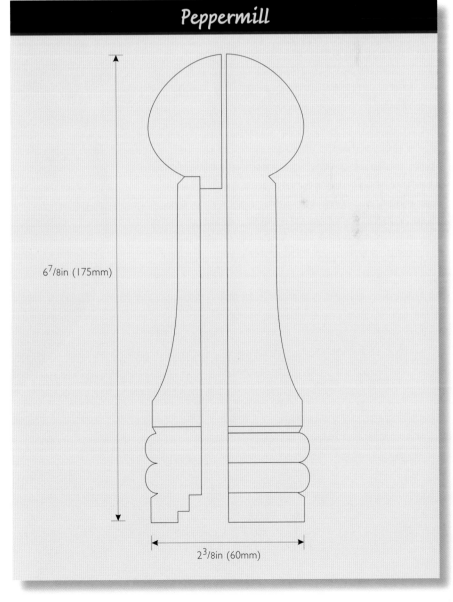

Peppermill

$6^7/8$in (175mm)

$2^3/8$in (60mm)

Hanging Pomander

For something different, chase a thread on the two halves of this hanging pomander.

Pomanders of any sort make very acceptable gifts and they are also one of the first things to be snapped up from your stall if you are making items for sale. Traditionally they are made to be freestanding, somewhat similar to an enclosed goblet, but I have always found the hanging type to be even more popular.

Being relatively small, pomanders also have the advantage of using up some of those offcuts that are too good to be thrown away, but too small for much else. Any sized piece will do; in this case I started with a yew log about 2^1/2in (63mm) diameter and 7in (180mm) long, but you can make much smaller ones, using whatever you have to hand.

Although a simple turning job, it is slightly complicated by the addition of the screwed lid, which actually is very easily chased by hand. If you feel you're not up to thread chasing, just make the lid a tight fit in the base. The addition of the thread also immediately limits your choice of timber species to fine-textured, close-grain material capable of taking a thread. However, because the thread is not going to be used on a regular basis, you can try using less conventional species, as the finished quality of the thread is not quite so critical. It is to be functional rather than ornamental.

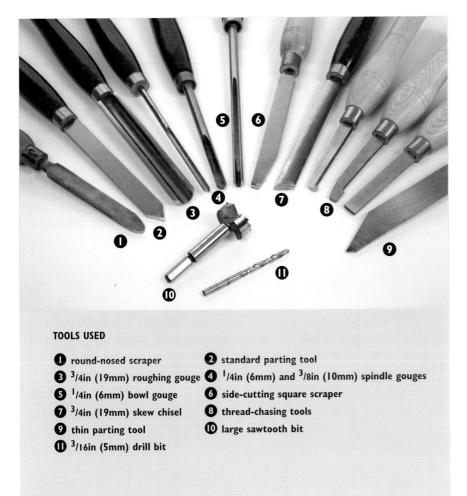

TOOLS USED

1. round-nosed scraper
2. standard parting tool
3. $^3/4$in (19mm) roughing gouge
4. $^1/4$in (6mm) and $^3/8$in (10mm) spindle gouges
5. $^1/4$in (6mm) bowl gouge
6. side-cutting square scraper
7. $^3/4$in (19mm) skew chisel
8. thread-chasing tools
9. thin parting tool
10. large sawtooth bit
11. $^3/16$in (5mm) drill bit

3 If the timber is very hard, it is better to use the roughing gouge well on its side. This reduces the width of the cut and therefore minimizes the load on the drive centre.

4 Use the parting tool with callipers to turn a gripping spigot at the tailstock end of the blank. To get the maximum grip, size it to be just slightly larger in diameter than the closed diameter of the chuck jaws.

1 Find the approximate centre of an odd-shaped blank like this, using a pair of dividers to scribe out the biggest circle.

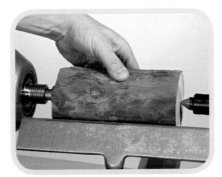

2 Initially mount the block between centres, spinning it by hand a few times to check for clearance over the toolrest – a very important step when you're using irregular-shaped pieces like this.

5 Use a skew chisel on its side to undercut the end of the blank and to form the required dove-tail over the length of the spigot. You won't get the chuck to grip securely, or accurately, unless the spigot and shoulder are formed cleanly like this.

6 Repeat the procedure, forming another spigot at the other end of the blank.

7 Transfer the blank to the chuck, gripping on what will be the bottom end of the pomander.

8 A fine parting tool is better for parting off the lid section as it minimizes the grain distortion when you put the two halves back together again later.

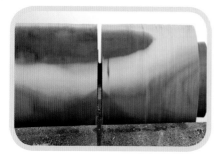

TIP: For deep parting cuts, remember to widen the groove slightly as you go in, to avoid the sides of the tool binding and burning.

9 Part right through after moving the tailstock back out of the way. If you are not confident about doing this, stop the lathe and make the final cut with a handsaw.

10 Use a sawtooth bit in the tailstock drill chuck to remove the bulk of the waste, pulling it back occasionally to stop the swarf jamming behind the bit.

CAUTION When withdrawing a drill held in the tailstock, keep hold of the chuck as you wind back, to ensure the arbor doesn't pull out of the tailstock barrel.

11 Start forming the outer profile, but don't shape down too far at the lower end of the pomander at this stage, or you will weaken it too much for the subsequent hollowing.

12 To open out the hole, use a square-ended side-cutting scraper, raising the toolrest slightly to get a definite trailing action. The two cutting edges allow you to either push the tool straight in, or move it out sideways.

13 Finish the hollowing, using a round-nosed scraper to blend the sides into the bottom in a nice curve.

14 Use a hook tool to form the definite undercut at the end of the female threaded section.

15 Reduce the lathe speed to about 400 rpm and start chasing the internal thread. Keep rotating the chaser in a clockwise direction, just kissing the wood to start with, then gradually applying more pressure as the thread starts to form.

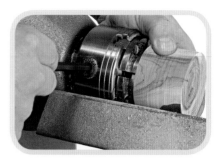

16 Remount the lid section on the lathe, gripping on the spigot you formed during the roughing-out process.

17 Turn down a short section onto which you can form the male thread. Although you can measure this diameter, it is better to fine tune it by regularly stopping the lathe and holding the two components together.

18 When they appear to match, chase the male thread, keeping the chaser angled slightly downwards to stop it snatching.

19 Try the lid for fit: if it is too big, reduce the diameter slightly with a parting tool and re-cut the thread. Don't try and reduce the diameter by pressing on harder with the chaser.

20 Hollow the underside of the lid slightly and drill a small hole to take the hanging ribbon.

21 Sand and polish this underside, then screw it up tight into the base section. The grain probably won't line up pefectly first time; while this may not be important with plain pieces of timber, with more decorative species it is important that the top and base do match up.

22 Remount the base in the chuck and keep trimming a fraction off the length and retrying the lid.

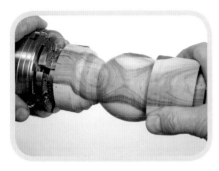

23 Keep taking a succession of these very light cuts until the grain on the lid and base line up perfectly.

24 With the lid back in place, start forming the finished profile of the lid – don't take massive cuts or you will risk stripping the thread.

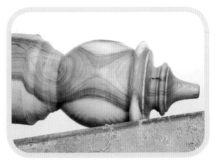

25 Complete the shaping of the lid, putting in the fine detail with a parting tool and ¹/₄in (6mm) spindle gouge.

26 Now use a pencil to scribe a line round the bowl section to mark the position of the holes.

27 If you have a dividing head, it is easy to set out the holes, otherwise use a set of dividers to step around the pencil line, adjusting the setting of the dividers until the start and finish points coincide.

28 Use a simple homemade drilling jig to ensure the holes are all in line and square. A brad point drill will usually start more accurately than an ordinary twist drill.

29 Sand and polish the outside of the lid section.

30 Remove the lid and clean up any break-out around the holes on the inside of the bowl using the round-nosed scraper.

31 Sand and polish the inside of the bowl, taking care not to damage the fine thread with the abrasive paper.

32 Complete as much of the shaping of the base as possible, leaving only a small amount of waste to be turned away later.

33 Grip a small offcut of suitable waste in the chuck and chase a thread to match that on the inside of the pomander base.

34 Remount the finished base section using this threaded waste piece as a temporary chuck.

35 Complete the shaping, taking fine delicate cuts with a small spindle gouge.

36 Sand and polish the base to match the lid section. The completed pomander just requires a small length of ribbon threading through the lid and knotting on the inside.

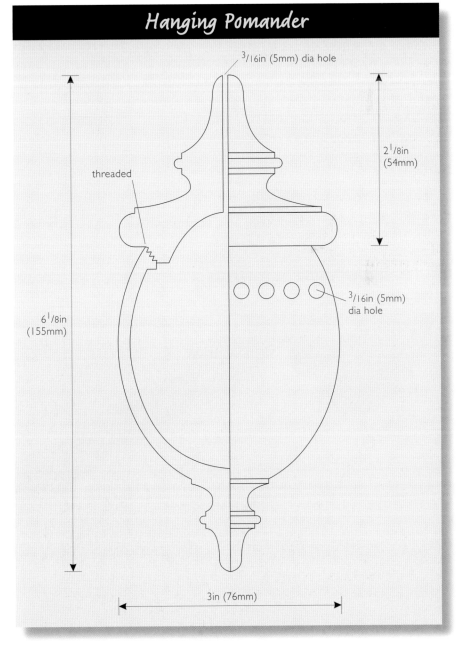

Hanging Pomander

3/16in (5mm) dia hole

2 1/8in (54mm)

threaded

3/16in (5mm) dia hole

6 1/8in (155mm)

3in (76mm)

Gavel

**Bring some order back into your house with this decorative gavel,
or just use it to tenderize your steaks!**

Strangely, a gavel is probably one of the most popular items in the professional woodturner's repertoire. It is amazing how many organizations there are that need some means of bringing their meetings to order. Once you have made one, word soon spreads and the orders should flow in.

It is a relatively simple project to make and you can make gavels as plain or as decorative as you like, as the only area needing careful attention is fitting the head of the gavel onto the handle. Remember that an over-zealous chairman trying to quell an unruly gathering may use it a bit over-enthusiastically and the head might loosen. You have two choices for fitting the head firmly: either bring the handle right through and wedge it like a conventional hammer, or wedge it internally using an adaptation of the

fox-wedged tenon found in general woodworking. I chose this latter option, as I think it is neater and it requires no hand finishing later. I have made hundreds of these gavels and never had one come loose yet, but you need to spend a bit of time to achieve a really accurate fit.

You don't need much in the way of materials. For this gavel you need a piece for the head 4 x 2^1/$_2$ x 2^1/$_2$in (100 x 63 x 63mm) and a piece 8 x 1^1/$_4$ x 1^1/$_4$in (203 x 32 x 32mm) for the handle. Here I used a piece of gonçalo alves with some really rich figuring, but anything strong will do, depending on the likely use. However, try to use timbers that are fine-grained enough to take the detail and hard enough to resist the inevitable wear. Among the cheaper home-grown timbers, ash and elm are both good candidates.

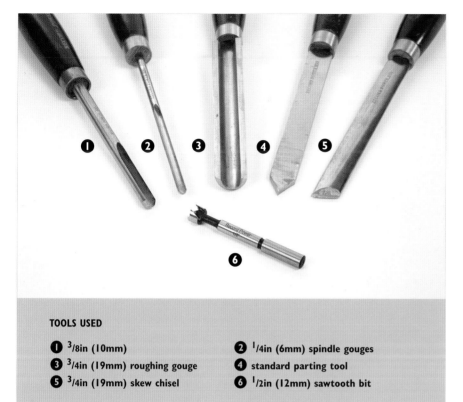

TOOLS USED

❶ ³/₈in (10mm)   ❷ ¹/₄in (6mm) spindle gouges
❸ ³/₄in (19mm) roughing gouge   ❹ standard parting tool
❺ ³/₄in (19mm) skew chisel   ❻ ¹/₂in (12mm) sawtooth bit

2 Drill a ¹/₂in (12mm) hole using a sawtooth bit accurately centred on the intersection of the diagonals. Keep withdrawing the bit as you drill to clear the swarf and prevent it overheating.

3 You can now either hold the block between centres, or in your chuck. I prefer the former as it allows me to complete most of the turning in one go and then just re-chuck for final cleaning up of the ends.

TIP: It is vital that the head sits squarely on the end of the handle, and this is down to really accurate drilling. It is much easier to drill before the block is turned, so make sure it is properly square and cut to length, and then find the centres of either end and on one face.

Ideally the drilling should be carried out on a drill press to get the handle square to the head in all planes. Start by setting the drill depth deep enough to allow plenty of penetration of the handle, but not so deep that the hole goes right through when the centre of the head is shaped away later.

4 Check the blank for clearance past the toolrest and make sure the rest and banjo are tightened up firmly.

5 You would normally need a lathe speed of about 2000 rpm for a small block like this, but nothing is critical, so set it at whatever feels comfortable to you.

6 Rough down the square using a ³/₄in (19mm) gouge. This will be very quick and easy at this speed and it is quite safe to work along the full length of such a small blank, rather than working out from either end.

7 When the blank is cylindrical, use a pencil to scribe a line round the centre. This should also coincide with the centre of the head hole.

8 Use the parting tool to cut in a small waste spigot at both ends, but make sure it is exactly the same width at either end.

9 Use dividers to set out the main detail points using the ends as the reference each time.

10 Callipers are essential to get matching diameters the same at either end, but take your time with this setting out, as the two halves need to be perfectly symmetrical for the finished head to look right.

11 Turn the head profile using a ¹/₄in (6mm) spindle gouge, taking light cuts to try and keep the design centred about the handle hole.

12 Work on the same bit of matching detail at either end, gradually working in towards the middle and stopping the lathe frequently to check that it's all still looking symmetrical.

13 **Tiny beads can be worked with the parting tool, by using it as a very small skew chisel.**

TIP: Finally 'sharpen' the detail by incising a tiny line at each main change of detail. This makes everything look much crisper.

14 **Complete as much as possible of the shaping at either end, leaving just a small pip to accommodate the centres.**

15 **Sand the surface very carefully to maintain the sharp edges to the detail. These are easily spoiled by careless sanding, so work down to about 400 grit paper, slowing the lathe speed down if the surface appears to be getting hot.**

16 **Rub in several coats of cellulose sanding sealer with the lathe stationary, flatting them down when dry with very fine abrasive – I used 800 grit.**

17 **Burnish the final; coat with 0000 wire wool. This leaves a super-smooth surface ready for polishing and is the only way to get an even, high gloss.**

18 **For small, decorative items my choice of finish is friction polish applied with a cloth as the lathe is revolving. Don't use too much, or the surface will end up quite streaky.**

19 **Using a strip of cloth to protect the polished surface, grip the finished head in some long jaws in the chuck. Tighten up firmly, but not so tight that it marks the surface.**

20 **Clean up the spigot left by the centre, cutting the bulk of it away with the parting tool, then cleaning up with a quick slice, using the skew chisel on its back.**

166

21 Sand and polish this surface, blending it into the existing polish on the outer edge to disguise the join (although this shouldn't really be visible).

22 The handle is next, so rough the blank down using the gouge and the lathe set at about 2500 rpm.

23 Set your callipers to the diameter of the sawtooth bit you used to drill the hole in the head.

24 Next, size down a small section at the end of the handle using the parting tool, until the callipers just slip over the diameter.

25 Check that this is a tight fit in the hole before you reduce the full length of the section to fit inside the head.

26 Complete the shaping of the handle – the roughing gouge and skew chisel are the best tools for long, gently curved sections like this.

27 With the bulk of the shaping complete, reverse the handle, gripping it at the headstock end in some small jaws in the chuck. Only grip on the section that is going to be hidden inside the head, so it doesn't matter if the surface is marked slightly by the jaws.

28 Complete the shaping at the top end of the handle, working down as close as possible to the centre, leaving just a small nib to take the tailstock centre.

29 Sand and polish the handle to match the head, then use the skew chisel to slice off the final supporting nib.

30 With the wood still gripped in the chuck, there should be enough support to sand and polish this final cut area, but do steady it with your fingers.

31 To assemble the head and handle, use a saw to make a cut down the centre of the end, to a length equivalent to just less than the depth of the hole in the head.

32 Cut a thin, tapering wedge equal in length to the saw cut and the same width as the handle diameter. Cover the wedge with glue, smear a little inside the hole in the head and push the two components together. The theory is that the wedge bottoms in the hole in the head and is then forced into the handle, opening out the saw cut and wedging it all in a really tight. It relies on accurate fitting of the components and the slightest of tapers on the wedge, but it has never failed me yet.

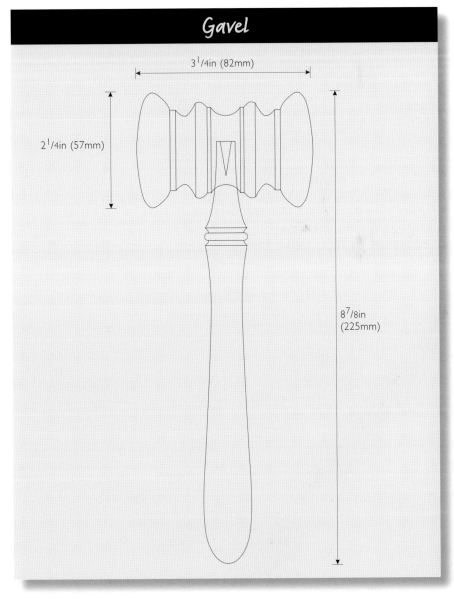

Gavel

3¹/4in (82mm)

2¹/4in (57mm)

8⁷/8in (225mm)

Suppliers

UK

Ashley Iles (Edge Tools Ltd)
East Kirkby
Spilsby
Lincs
PE2 4DD
Tel: +44 (0)1790 763372
www.ashleyiles.co.uk

Axminster Power Tool Centre
Chard Street
Axminster
Devon
EX13 5DZ
Tel: +44 (0)1297 33656
www.axminster.co.uk

D&M Tools
73–81 Heath Road
Twickenham
Middlesex
TW1 4AW
Tel: +44 (0)2088 923813
www.dmtools.co.uk

Hegner UK Ltd
Units 1 and 2, North Crescent
Diplocks Way
Hailsham
Essex
BN27 3JF
Tel: +44 (0)12323 442440
www.hegner.co.uk

Henry Taylor Tools Ltd
The Forge, Peacock Estate
Livesey Street
Sheffield
S6 2BL
Tel: +44 (0)1142 340282
www.henrytaylortools.co.uk

Peter Child
The Old Hyde
Little Yeldham
Nr Halstead
Essex
CO9 4QT
Tel: +44 (0)1787 237291
www.peterchild.co.uk

Record Power Ltd
Unit B, Adelphi Way
Ireland Industrial Estate
Staveley
Chesterfield
S43 3LS
Tel: +44 (0)1246 561520
www.recordpower.co.uk

Robert Sorby
Athol Road
Sheffield
S8 0PA
Tel: +44 (0)1142 250700
www.robert-sorby.co.uk

Timberline
Unit 7, Munday Industrial Estate
58–66 Morley Road
Tonbridge
Kent
TN7 1RP
Tel: +44 (0)1732 355626
www.exotichardwoods.co.uk

Turners Retreat
Snape Lane
Harworth
North Nottinghamshire
DN11 8NE
Tel: +44 (0)1302 744344
www.turners-retreat.co.uk

Whitmore's Timber
Main Road
Claybrooke Magna
Nr Lutterworth
Leics.
LE17 5AQ
Tel: +44 (0)1455 209121
www.whitmores.co.uk

Yandle and Sons Ltd
Hurst Works
Martock
Somerset
TA12 6JU
Tel: +44 (0)1935 822207
www.yandles.co.uk

AUSTRALIA

Vicmarc Machinery
52 Grice Street
Clontarf
Queensland 4350
Australia
Tel: 00 61 7 007 3284 3103
www.vicmarc.com

CANADA

Oneway Manufacturing
241 Monteith Ave
Stratford
Ontario
N5A 2P6
Tel: 001 (800)565-7288
www.oneway.ca

USA

Craft Supplies USA
Provo
Utah 84608
USA
Tel: 001 (801)373-0917
www.woodturnerscatalogue.com

Glaser Engineering Co.
PO Box 95
El Segundo
CA 90245
USA
Tel: 001 (310)823-7128
www.glaserhitec.com

Glossary

Air-dried Timber that has reached its equilibrium moisture content with the outdoor environment.

Annual ring The layer of wood that a tree gains in a single year, made up of a band of earlywood and a band of latewood.

Banjo The part of the lathe that supports the toolrest on the lathe bed. It slides in all directions along the bed to allow positioning of the toolrest. Sometimes referred to as the saddle.

Bark The protective outer layer of the tree's trunk, including the inner living bark and the outer dead bark.

Bead Rounded convex feature on a piece of turning, usually semicircular but maybe more pointed.

Between centres The distance between the drive and tailstock centre points.

Bevel The area immediately behind the cutting edge of the tool which may be flat, hollow or convex.

Blank A prepared piece of timber for turning. Long, thin pieces are normally referred to as spindle blanks, squat circular pieces are termed bowl blanks.

Board A piece of timber with wane on at least one of the edges.

Board foot A unit of measurement of timber equivalent in volume to a piece 12in (305mm) square and 1in (25mm) thick.

Bole A tree stem or trunk large enough for conversion into boards.

Burr An outgrowth on the side of a tree caused by a mass of small, growing shoots. The resulting jumbled grain produces highly decorative figure when sliced through.

Catch Chance contact between the revolving workpiece and the tool edge, usually leading to damage to the workpiece.

Centres Provide drive and support for long, thin workpieces when held between the headstock and tailstock.

Chasers Tools used for cutting screw threads freehand. Usually supplied in pairs, male for the external thread and female for the internal.

Checks A lengthwise separation of wood cells along the grain as a result of uneven shrinkage, commonly seen on end-grain surfaces.

Conditioning Exposing timber to a controlled relative humidity to achieve the required moisture content.

Conifer Trees of the genus gymnosperms, characterized by needle-like leaves and which are usually evergreen.

Counterbore tool Modified four-pronged drive centre with a $5/16$in (8mm) central spigot to support pre-drilled lamp blanks.

Cove Rounded concave feature on a piece of turning.

Crotch Highly figured wood taken from the area where a branch joins the main trunk.

Cubic foot Unit of measurement of timber equivalent to a piece 12 × 12 × 12in (305 × 305 × 305mm).

Dead centre Solid steel Morse-taper centre for the tailstock, which is fixed rather than revolving with the work. Can cause burning if over-tightened.

Deciduous A type of tree where the leaves fall off after the yearly growth cycle, typical of most hardwoods, but not all.

Density The weight of wood substance per unit volume.

Diffuse porous Hardwood species when the vessels formed throughout the growth ring are of uniform size and distribution.

Dig-in Severe catch resulting from the tool being presented wrongly to the revolving work. Often causes major damage to the work and may even cause injury to the turner.

Drive centre Pronged centre on a Morse taper that fits into the headstock to provide drive to the work. Normally two or four pronged.

Drying defects Irregularities caused by incorrect drying procedures that damage or otherwise affect the strength and quality of the timber.

Earlywood A band of quick-grown cells produced early in the growing season and characterized by larger cells with lower density.

End checks A drying defect, caused by the ends of the boards drying faster than the rest of the timber, that can be reduced by end sealing.

End grain The cross-sectional surface of a board.

End sealing Coating the ends of boards to slow down the rate of drying and so minimize end checking.

Extractives Substances deposited in wood as it changes from sapwood to heartwood. They impart colour and resistance to decay.

Faceplate Used to hold work to the headstock when it is impractical to support it with the tailstock.

Figure The distinctive pattern on the longitudinal wood surface caused by anatomical features, defects and the orientation of the log during cutting.

Fillet Small flat area of detail in a piece of turning. Sometimes referred to as a shoulder.

Flute U-shaped depression along the inside of gouges.

Grain The direction of the wood fibres relative to the long axis of the tree trunk.

Green Fresh-cut or unseasoned material with a moisture content above the fibre saturation point.

Grit A system of classifying the particle size on abrasive materials. The lower the number the coarser the grit.

Hardwood Wood cut from broadleaved trees in the botanical classification of angiosperms.

Headstock The main part of the lathe containing the drive shaft, motor and speed-change mechanism.

Heartwood Timber from the central portion of the trunk is often darker due to the deposition of extractives.

Heel The area of support at the opposite end of the bevel to the cutting edge.

HSS High-speed steel.

Hygroscopic Having the ability to absorb water.

Inboard This is the end of the main spindle over the bed. Some lathes have both inboard and outboard spindle ends.

Kiln-dried timber Material which has been dried in a kiln to a specified moisture content, usually well below what can be attained by air-drying.

Knot A section of a twig or branch that has been overgrown by the expanding girth of the bole. May be live or dead.

Latewood The section of the growth ring formed after the earlywood, usually containing smaller cells with thicker walls and a higher density.

Live centre A tailstock centre that revolves with the workpiece, so eliminating any danger of burning the work. Also called a revolving centre.

Long-hole boring Forming the long hole down the length of a lamp blank. Usually accomplished with the $5/16$in (8mm) long-hole auger.

Moisture content The weight of water in a piece of timber expressed as a percentage of the dry weight.

Moisture meter An electronic device used to give an instant readout of the moisture content.

Morse taper A universal system for attaching accessories using push-fit tapers. Used in both the headstock and tailstock for the centres and other accessories such as drill chucks and boring bits.

Ogee A classic S-shaped detail on a turned profile.

Outboard The left-hand end of the lathe spindle may protrude through the headstock to allow the turning of big-diameter items. This outboard thread has to be left-handed to prevent the work unscrewing.

PEG Polyethylene glycol used as a method of stabilizing wet timber.

Pith The small, soft and spongy core at the very centre of the tree. Maybe hollow in some species.

Plank A piece of timber with both edges square.

Pummel A square section on a turned workpiece.

Quarter sawn Boards cut with the growth rings as near as possible at 90° to the face. Used to reveal decorative figuring in species with heavy rays.

Ray Flat bands of tissue orientated perpendicular to the trunk for transport of food materials across the stem.

Relative humidity Ratio of the amount of water actually present in the air relative to the amount that it could theoretically hold.

Revolving centre A tailstock centre fitted with bearings so that it revolves with the timber and eliminates any chance of burning the work.

Ring porous Hardwood where the quick-growing earlywood vessels are very much larger than the later-grown vessels, resulting in the distinctive annual ring.

Saddle See Banjo.

Sap Water in the tree containing dissolved food substances.

Sapwood The active timber comprising of the most recent annual rings; it is usually lighter-coloured than the heartwood.

Seasoning The process of drying wood to a usable state.

Shake A timber defect where the wood separates lengthwise, often along the growth rings, as in a ring shake.

Shrinkage The changes in dimension that occur in a piece of wood as it dries below the fibre saturation point.

Softwood Wood from coniferous trees in the botanical group called gymnosperms.

Spalted Partially rotten wood that exhibits highly decorative colouration due to the fungal zone lines.

Specific gravity The ratio of the weight of a piece of wood relative to the weight of an equal volume of water.

Spigot A dowel or pin on one end of a workpiece, usually used for jointing two pieces together or for holding by means of a chuck.

Spindle nose The threaded section of the main lathe spindle onto which are screwed accessories such as chucks. The spindle nose is usually bored with a Morse taper.

Split Separation of the wood tissue that extends completely through a board, usually on the end.

Stickers Small pieces of wood, normally about ¾in (19mm) square, used to separate wet boards for drying.

Surface checks Shallow cracks in the timber surface, caused by uneven drying or exposure to heat.

Swing Denotes the biggest diameter workpiece that can be turned over the bed.

Swinging head Where the headstock swivels round on the bed, allowing you to turn bigger items clear of the bed restrictions. Normally requires the use of an additional toolrest support.

Tailstock The opposite end of the bed to the headstock, the tailstock moves along the length of the bed and houses an adjustable barrel for holding work between centres.

Texture Describes the size of cells in the tissue make-up, ranging from very fine to coarse.

Toolrest A T-shaped rest for the cutting tools that fits into the banjo.

Trunk The main section of the tree producing the bulk of the timber.

Woodturning Courses

John Berkeley
11 Faringdon Avenue
Lutterworth
Leics
LE 17 4DJ
Tel: +44 (0)1455 557938
john@johnberkeley.co.uk

John Davis
The Old Stables
Chilbolton Down Farm
Stockbridge
Hampshire
SO20 6BU
Tel: +44 (0)1264 811070
www.johndaviswoodturning.co.uk

Melvyn Firmager
Nut Tree Farm
Stoughton Cross
Wedmore
Somerset
BS28 4PQ
Tel: +44 (0)1934 712404
m@melvynfirmager.co.uk

Brian Hannan
Unit 7
Viables Craft Centre
Harrow Way
Basingstoke
RG22 4BJ
Tel: +44 (0)1256 811911

W. L .West & Sons Ltd
Selham
Petworth
West Sussex
GU28 0PJ
Tel: +44 (0)1978 861611
www.wlwest.co.uk

Yandle & Sons Ltd
Hurst Works
Martock
Somerset
TA12 6JU
Tel: +44 (0)1935 822207
www.yandles.co.uk

Record Power Ltd.
Unit B, Adelphi Way
Ireland Industrial Estate
Staveley
Chesterfield
S43 3LS
Tel: +44 (0)1246 561520
www.recordpower.co.uk

Axminster Power Tool Centre
Chard Street
Axminster
Devon
EX13 5DZ
Tel: +44 (0)1297 33656
www.axminster.co.uk

Peter Child
The Old Hyde
Little Yeldham
Nr Halstead
Essex
CO9 4QT
Tel: +44 (0)1787 238522
www.peterchild.co.uk

Stiles & Bates
Upper Farm
Church Hill
Sutton
Dover
Kent
CT15 5DF
Tel: +44 (0)1304 366360
www.stilesandbates.co.uk

Turners Retreat
Snape Lane
Harworth
North Nottinghamshire
DN11 8NE
Tel: +44 (0)1302 744344
www.turners-retreat.co.uk

Gregory Moreton
47 Wood End
Common Road
Claygate
Esher
Surrey
KT10 0HU
Tel: +44 (0)1372 467692
www.LearnToTurn.co.uk

Nick Arnull
Latrigg
Horsford
Norfolk
NR10 3DB
Tel: +44 (0)1603 710722
enquiries@nickarnullwoodturner.co.uk

Ted Farrow
76 Langford Cottage
Lavant
Chichester
West Sussex
PO18 0JR
Tel: +44 (0)1243 527242
woodturner@tedfarrow.co.uk

About the Author

Alan Holtham has been involved in all aspects of woodworking for over 30 years. After graduating with a degree in Forestry and Wood Science he established a specialist woodworking business that grew to supply tools and machinery to customers all over the world, as well as importing and processing timber for both retail and wholesale customers.

After 20 years at the 'sharp end' of retailing, he decided to take a step back and concentrate on sharing his accumulated knowledge and experience, setting up a dedicated film studio and workshop in 2000. Initially making instructional and promotional videos covering all aspects of woodworking machinery, the media business grew rapidly and Alan has now written hundreds of magazine articles and continues to write and present a variety of woodworking programmes on DVD.

He has appeared on many woodworking programmes on television and regularly demonstrates tools and techniques on behalf of major machinery and tool manufacturers.

Alan's simple, down-to-earth approach fronts a personal ambition to demystify woodworking and bring it back as a mainstream interest for all, but particularly for youngsters whom he feels have been sadly neglected by an education system that places little credibility on teaching practical hand skills. His book, *How to Season and Dry Your Own Wood*, was published by GMC Publications in 2009.

Index

Names of projects are printed in **bold**.

To place an order, or to request a catalogue, please contact:

GMC Publications
Castle Place, 166 High Street, Lewes, East Sussex
BN7 1XU, United Kingdom

Tel: +44 (0)1273 488005 Fax: +44 (0)1273 402866
Website: www.gmcbooks.com

Orders by credit card are accepted